MINIATURE
TEDDY BEAR
COLLECTION

JULIE K. OWEN

David & Charles

DEDICATION

To my children, James and Hilary, with love.

A DAVID & CHARLES BOOK

First published in the UK in 2002
by David & Charles
ISBN 0 7153 1128 X (hardback)

Distributed in North America
by F&W Publications, Inc.
4700 E. Galbraith Road
Cincinnati, OH 45236
ISBN 0 7153 1269 3 (paperback)

Photography by Alan Duns
Patterns and diagrams by Ethan Danielson
Original book design by Bridgewater Books Company
Layout by Visual Image
Printed in China
for David & Charles
Brunel House   Newton Abbot   Devon

CONTENTS

INTRODUCTION

The year 2002 is the 100th anniversary of the teddy bear. These cuddly creatures are now so much a part of our heritage that it is hard to conceive of a time before bears but the story of their conception goes like this. It was on November 15th 1902 when President Theodore Roosevelt attended a bear hunt in Mississippi and his only chance to kill was a bear cub cornered, exhausted and tied to a tree. He refused to shoot in such unfair circumstances and the incident was illustrated the following day in the Washington Post by cartoonist Clifford Barryman. The cartoon drew a lot of attention and the following day shopkeeper Morris Michtom placed two bears in his window made by his wife Rose along with a cutting of the cartoon. The toy was very popular and Michtom wrote to Roosevelt asking permission to call them Teddy's Bear. Roosevelt replied: 'I don't think my name is likely to be worth much in the toy bear business but you are welcome to use it'. Little did he know how popular the teddy would be.

With increasing interest in teddy bears more and more people are now keen to make their own and as miniature bears take up a lot less room than their full-size counterparts they are becoming even more popular. Collectors who are short of space are now turning their attention to miniature bears too and with their high standard of workmanship they are becoming very collectable. Being small they can be tucked in a pocket as a good-luck charm or they can be personalised to make wonderful gifts. As the bears are all stitched by hand it is a very portable hobby: once the pieces have been cut out, you can sit and sew them anywhere. It is very satisfying when you complete a bear – no two ever turn out quite the same and each has its very own character. So have a go, have fun and make a friend.

MATERIALS AND TOOLS

'Look for the bear necessities, those simple bear necessities...'
DISNEY'S 'THE JUNGLE BOOK'

Making miniature bears is very easy to begin because you do not need to spend a fortune to get started. However, there are a few special tools which will make the job easier and which will enable you to make better bears. These are listed here.

FABRIC

When choosing fabric for miniature bear making it is important that it does not fray. As the bears are so small, only a tiny seam allowance is given and therefore if the fabric is too loosely woven it will fray very easily and your seams won't hold. It is possible to treat fabric to prevent fraying when you work with it (see below), but beginners will find standard miniature bear fabric easier to work with. For people new to miniature bear making it is also best to avoid fabric that has a very short pile or is completely flat as it can be more difficult to obtain good results when closing seams.

Upholstery fabric is an excellent choice. It has a firm backing which does not stretch when stuffed and does not usually fray. The length of the pile varies.

Pure mohair for miniature bears is available in different pile lengths starting from $\frac{1}{8}$in (3mm). Again, it comes in a wide range of colours and you can also dye it yourself or buy mohair that has been hand dyed. Sparse mohair is also available which gives the bears a different, slightly worn look.

Velvet can be used to make miniature bears but it usually frays badly. However, it can be treated before you start sewing (see below).

Felt is used for the nursery toys at the back of this book. It tends to stretch when you stuff it but you can prevent this by applying iron-on interfacing to one side before cutting out your pieces.

Silk or cotton can be used by the more experienced bear maker if the fabric has a small print, but it may be necessary to apply an iron-on interfacing to give a firmer backing and also to treat the edges to avoid fraying.

Ultra suede is often used for paws and pads. This is fine suede which is available in a wide range of colours.

Suedette is a synthetic fabric which can also be used for paws and pads. This is usually thicker than ultra suede and therefore quite bulky.

Alternative finishes Many of the fabrics suitable for making miniature bears are available with a distressed finish which is obtained by a steaming process in the manufacture of the fabric and gives an old, well-worn effect. Crushed velvet is an example of this.

Fray prevention There are several products available which help prevent fraying. Fray Check crystals are particularly good because you can treat the whole fabric before cutting out, (see Suppliers, page 95). Alternatively, with liquid Fray Check you paint round the design on the fabric and allow it to dry. This seals the fabric prior to cutting out. Other options are to use clear nail varnish or PVA glue diluted with an equal part of water. Apply these to the cut edges of your fabric pieces.

There are many miniature bear suppliers who will send bear fabrics and other specialist items by post (see Suppliers, page 95 and more can also be found in teddy

bear magazines). For a nominal fee companies
will usually send small swatches of their fabrics.

THREADS

Polyester-cotton general-purpose sewing thread is ideal
for stitching miniature bears. Use a colour which matches
the backing of your fabric.

Nylon monofil 'invisible' thread is initially more difficult
to use than polyester-cotton because you can't see where
you have sewn – or what you are sewing with. If you
thread your needle with it and then knot the two ends
together it avoids the problem of your needle coming off
all the time. Do not use it to close seams with ladder stitch
because it does not give a very good finish. However, it
is very useful when dressing or making accessories for
the bears.

Extra-strong nylon thread is used mainly for thread
jointing in miniature bears. It is usually available in black,
brown or white but as it will not be visible when the bear
is completed it does not matter which colour you use.

Stranded embroidery thread is used for noses and claws
– usually black. For miniature bears you generally only
need to use one strand at a time.

Beeswax This is available from haberdashery shops. It is
a hard block of wax and you run your thread across it to
strengthen the thread before sewing with it. It also helps
prevent the thread from getting tangled.

FILLINGS

Polyester filling is most often used for miniature
bears because it enables you to obtain a firm, even finish.

Glass bead filling is used to add weight. As you can't
actually mould it into shape, it is usually put in the body
only. If you do want to use it in the limbs you must use
cotter pin joints because the thread jointing system does
not hold in place. Alternatively, insert some polyester
filling at the top of the limbs where the thread joints will
go. A syringe provides a good, clean way of stuffing the
bear when using glass bead filling.

Steel shot is also sometimes used to give weight to a bear.
It is good to use because you can actually feel the 'pellet'
filling. Be sure it is stainless steel or has been treated and
is labelled 'rust free', otherwise it may rust with time.

COMPONENTS

Joints A cotter pin joint consists of a pin with two round
discs or washers. There are two types of cotter pins: one
with a round top and one with a 'T' shaped top. The 'T'
cotter pins are usually used for jointing the limbs of
miniature bears; the round-head cotter pins can be used

for jointing the head. When a measurement is given this usually refers to the diameter of the round discs. Miniature bear joints are available in different sizes starting from ¼in (6mm) and are usually sold in sets of five.

Eyes Black onyx beads are available in various sizes, starting at 1/16in (1.5mm). They are usually round and bed into the bear's head very well. Glass eyes on wire are available in small sizes from specialist suppliers which enable you to use two-colour eyes. They are usually amber with a black pupil. Sometimes the wires are already cut and the loops formed, ready to attach to your bear. It is necessary to pinch the loops before you attach the eyes and sometimes they can shatter when you do this (see page 44). Small black glass embroidery beads can also be used.

Armature By inserting armature into the limbs of a miniature bear it is possible to pose the bear in a particular position. It is only necessary to use armature in the limbs that will be posed. The technique uses galvanised wire and washer replacements. Armature components are available from The Great British Bear Company.

MINIATURE BEAR TOOLS

Many of the things you need to make miniature bears will be found in your workbox including glass-headed pins, thimble and stiletto. However, there are also a few special tools you will need:

*Sewing needle*s Fine needles are recommended for the small stitches needed for small bears. No. 10 or No. 11 sharps are ideal. A darning needle is required for thread jointing and inserting the eyes.

Scissors Two pairs of scissors are required: one pair of small, sharp, pointed scissors which should only be used for cutting fabric and threads and never used to cut anything else; and another pair for cutting paper and card when making templates. (If you use your fabric scissors to cut paper you will blunt them.)

Round-nose pliers are required to turn the cotter pin joints. Alternatively use a cotter key.

Cotter key is used for turning cotter pin joints.

Curved artery forceps are invaluable when turning the bear's limbs right side out. Insert the forceps into the limb and lock them to hold the fabric before you pull it through. Take care not to pull any pile off the fabric but if you do, apply a small dab of glue to the bald patch and reattach the pile. Alternatively, make a new limb.

Dental tweezers have a curved end which enables you to put the stuffing exactly where you want it.

(These three tools are all available from the Great British Bear Company, see page 95.)

A *teasel brush* is used when your miniature bear is complete to remove any pile that has been trapped in the seams. These are available from haberdashery departments or from specialist miniature bear suppliers.

A *sleeve board* is like a long, narrow 'mini' ironing board and is very useful when pressing small clothes.

Glue It is preferable to stitch rather than glue because it is usually more permanent and using glue can sometimes look messy or make the fabric very stiff. However, when making accessories there are times when it is necessary to glue, in which case the glue sold by dolls' house suppliers is recommended. Try Hi-Tack, an all-purpose glue which dries clear and is flexible. You'll also need a solid *glue stick* for gluing your tracings of the pattern pieces onto the card to make your templates.

Thin cardboard (postcard or a cereal packet) is required for making templates.

Gel pens are used for drawing round the templates because they do not smudge and the ink does not come off onto your hands. Choose a colour which will be easy to see on your fabric but is not so dark that it will show through onto the right side.

GENERAL STITCHING INSTRUCTIONS

'It was brown in colour, a rather dirty brown, and it was wearing a most odd-looking hat with a wide brim.'

'A BEAR CALLED PADDINGTON' BY MICHAEL BOND

Before you begin making your bear take time to read the following general instructions first. You will make a much better bear and find the process much simpler and more straightforward. You'll be working on a very small scale, so it's vital that you cut out all the pieces and stitch them very accurately. This chapter tells you how and provides some very useful pointers on assembling your bear. With such a wide variety of fabrics available, depending on the fabric you choose your bear will often look quite different from those illustrated. This is not because it has turned out wrong, but because your bear is personal to you.

MAKING YOUR TEMPLATES

Making accurate templates is very important because as the pieces are so small any deviation will affect the finished bear. You have to stitch very accurately too, and you'll find this much easier if you mark the stitching line on the fabric, rather than the cutting line. You do this by drawing around templates. To make templates from the patterns carefully trace each piece and glue the tracing onto a piece of card. Add all markings to the templates and label them, then cut round each card piece with your scissors. Store the templates in a small plastic bag and label with the name, source and size.

POSITIONING THE PATTERN

Check your fabric to find the direction of the pile by gently running your hand down the fabric in different directions. When your hand runs smoothly, that is the direction of the pile. The pattern pieces should each be positioned on the reverse side of the fabric with the arrow pointing in the direction of the pile.

CUTTING OUT THE FABRIC

Do not pin the templates onto the fabric because they are too small – hold each template in position and draw round it with a gel pen, leaving gaps between pieces for the seam allowances, as shown. The pen line indicates the sewing line, not the cutting line, so do not cut on the line. Use small, sharp fabric scissors to cut carefully around all the pieces approximately ⅛in (3mm) outside the line – this is your seam allowance.

USEFUL STITCHES

You only need to know how to work a few simple stitches to complete the miniature bears in this book. Most seams are stitched with ordinary backstitch and any gaps remaining after stuffing are closed with ladder stitch. You'll also need to know how to work satin stitch for the bears' noses. Other stitches you may need for specific projects are blanket stitch, French knots, oversewing, running stitch and slipstitch. All these are explained and demonstrated here.

Backstitch Use this to stitch all seams unless otherwise directed. Starting one stitch from the beginning of the seam, bring your needle out at A. Take it back through at B and bring it out to the left of A at C, making sure the stitches are small and even. Work the next stitch by taking the needle through at A and out at D, then continue working in the same way with small, even stitches.

Blanket Stitch Create one straight stitch to start the line neatly by bringing the needle up at A. Go down at B and up at C (immediately to the side of A). Leave the required space and take the needle down at D and up at E, with the thread running behind the needle. Draw the needle through the fabric to form the stitch. The stitch pattern is formed by repeating this sequence. Try not to pull too tightly when drawing the thread through as this may cause puckering.

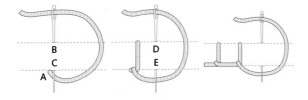

Double Stitches These are used to secure your work. Simply work back over the previous stitch, bringing the needle and thread through the same fabric holes as before.

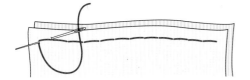

This is usually done at the beginning and end of a seam and at certain points where extra strength is needed, such as at the bear's neck.

French Knots Use these either separately or in clusters to create a three-dimensional effect. Bring the needle up at A and draw the thread through the fabric. Wind the thread around the needle by taking the thread over and under the needle. Take the thread back over and under the needle for a second time. Pull the thread gently so that it tightens around the needle (but not too tightly). Hold the thread to stop the stitch unravelling on the needle and insert the needle at B, close to A. Pull the thread through the fabric to form the knot.

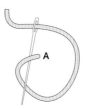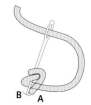

Ladder Stitch Use this to close all gaps in the seams. It enables you to stitch two pieces together on the right side, almost invisibly, and it is a most important stitch in miniature bear making. Use thread to match your miniature bear fabric. Starting with a knot, bring your needle out at A and go across into B, come out at C and go in at D. Continue in this way, stopping after every two or three stitches to pull the thread tight, and tucking in the raw edges as you go. To knot off neatly see the tip in the box, right.

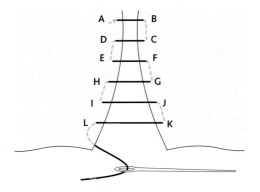

Oversewing Use this stitch, also called overcast stitch, to join two fabric edges together, working from the right side. Working from right to left, pick up a little of one fabric.

Catch the other fabric and then pass the needle through to the first fabric in one movement, as shown. Repeat to stitch the seam.

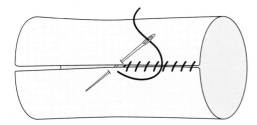

Running Stitch Use this stitch to gather up fabric, both on the bears and for their outfits. Working from right to left, 'run' the needle in and out of the fabric to create small, evenly spaced stitches, as shown. If you are working running stitch to gather up fabric, especially if it is fairly thick fabric, it is often best to use a double thread for strength.

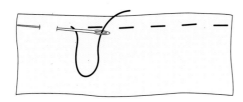

Satin Stitch This is used for filling in the bears' noses. It is usually done with one strand of black stranded embroidery thread. Bring the needle up at A and insert it at B. Bring it up again at C (next to A) and insert it at D (next to B). Continue in the same way to fill in the area required with close stitches that butt up together.

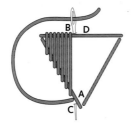

Slipstitch Use this strong stitch to finish hems or to close the opening between two edges. Working from right to left, bring the needle up on one side at A and insert it in the other side ⅟₁₆in (1.5mm) further along at B. Bring the needle out a short distance along at C and then cross to the other side again ⅟₁₆in (1.5mm) further along at D. Continue in this way to the end.

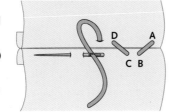

Helpful hints and pointers

✳ The line drawn round each template is the sewing line unless stated otherwise in the instructions – cut out the pieces approximately ⅛in (3mm) outside this line. When transferring a pattern onto dark fabric use a white or silver pencil or gel pen. Alternatively, try a dressmaker's chalk pencil although you have to be careful because this rubs off easily.

✳ Before stitching, place the pieces together with right sides facing and secure with just one pin or a single tacking stitch. This holds the pieces together while you sew the seam.

✳ Sew all pieces together with right sides facing, stitching on the pen line unless stated otherwise in the instructions, then turn right sides out. You may find it helpful to tack the end of the seam before you start to make sure you get a good fit.

✳ Use a piece of beeswax to run your thread across before you start sewing. This helps avoid the thread from getting tangled and also strengthens it. Do not use beeswax when embroidering the nose or when inserting the eyes, only when backstitching the pieces together and when closing the seams with ladder stitch.

✳ Do not sew too close to the fabric edge or you may find that the stitches pull away when stuffed – holes in seams can be difficult to repair. This is a particular problem with fabrics which fray easily such as mohair.

✳ Once you have completed ladder stitching a seam tie a knot in the thread but do not pull it tight. Insert your needle back into the knot and run the knot down to the surface of the fabric. Insert your needle back into the hole you came out of and bring it out well away from where you finished stitching. Give a sharp tug on the needle and you'll hear the knot pop through into the bear. Cut off the thread close to the fabric.

✳ When backstitching finish your thread by going over your last stitch again and then weave the needle back along the previous stitches and cut off.

✳ Remember, small bears need small stitches and, as you are working on a tiny scale, any deviation from the pattern will change the shape or proportions of your bear, so work carefully when cutting and stitching.

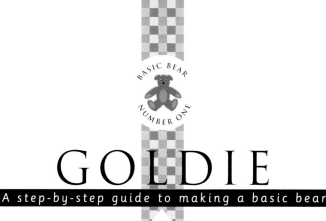

BASIC BEAR
NUMBER ONE

GOLDIE

A step-by-step guide to making a basic bear

'A bear is for life, not just for Christmas.'

RICHARD CARTER

Goldie is a young bear made from long-pile American upholstery fabric with matching ultra suede paws and pads. He is quite easy to make and an excellent bear for beginners. His sparkling black eyes suggest a lively intelligence and he may get into some mischief if you aren't careful, but his sunny smile reveals that he's not really a very naughty bear. His jointed head and limbs enable him to get about all over the place, to sit and to stand, but if you like you can make him even more versatile by giving him armatured limbs, following the instructions for Amelia on page 36.

Goldie is the first basic bear. Make him as he is to start with, especially if you have never made a bear before, and then try a few adaptations. For example, you could make him in an alternative fabric, try giving him a new nose and mouth or trim him differently as a present – he makes a wonderful wedding anniversary gift, for instance (see page 18). However, be warned that he is a very difficult bear to part with, so you may need to make two and keep one for yourself.

You will need

- ✢ 6 x 9in (15 x 23cm) piece of miniature bear fabric (American upholstery fabric, short-pile mohair or soft upholstery fabric)
- ✢ Matching ultra suede for paws and pads
- ✢ General-purpose sewing thread to match bear fabric
- ✢ Black extra-strong nylon thread for attaching eyes
- ✢ Black stranded embroidery thread for the nose
- ✢ Black ultra suede for the nose
- ✢ Darning and fine sharp needles
- ✢ Polyester filling
- ✢ Pair of tiny (2mm) black beads for eyes
- ✢ Four ¼in (6mm) 'T' pin fibreboard cotter pin joints
- ✢ One ¼in (6mm) round pin fibreboard cotter pin joint
- ✢ Stiletto
- ✢ Ribbon for trimming Goldie

FINISHED SIZE
3¾IN (9.5CM)

Making Goldie

Trace the pieces for Goldie from page 15 and use them to make card templates (see page 9). Transfer the paws and foot pads onto a single layer of ultra suede and cut out, adding an $\frac{1}{8}$in (3mm) seam allowance around each piece. Transfer the remaining pieces onto the wrong side of a single layer of miniature bear fabric with the arrow on the pattern pointing in the direction of the fabric pile. Make sure you transfer the joint position marks onto the two body pieces and the appropriate arms and legs – this is most important. Cut out the pieces, adding an $\frac{1}{8}$in (3mm) seam allowance around each one. Make the bear following the instructions below, using backstitch for joining pieces and ladder stitch for closing seams (see page 10).

2 *Joining the arms* With right sides together, sew the straight edge of an ultra suede paw to the straight edge of each inner arm. Then, with right sides together, sew each inner arm to an outer arm, beginning at A and working round the top, side and lower edge to B. Turn right sides out, turning the top part first – the paw will follow through.

1 *Joining the body* Pin the two body pieces together with right sides facing. Beginning at A with a double stitch, sew right round to B, being sure to stitch exactly on the pen line. Work a double stitch to finish, then knot the thread on the wrong side and trim off the thread end. Turn right sides out.

TIP – Using forceps for turning the limbs

Ideally, you should use bear forceps for turning the limbs, but if you don't have this tool an orange stick (used in nail manicure) can be used. For details of where to obtain bear forceps see Suppliers, page 95.

3 *Joining the legs* Pin the leg pieces together in pairs with right sides facing. Take two leg pieces and backstitch from A up round the top of the leg to B; leave the thread attached. Sew from C to D and knot and trim off the thread.

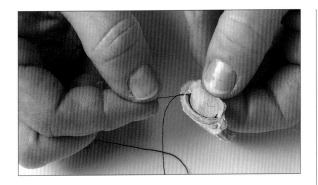

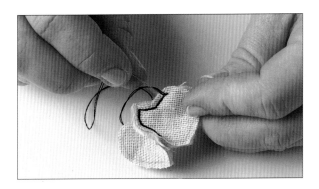

4 *Attaching the foot pads* Fold each foot pad in half lengthways and mark the centre at each end. Line up the slightly narrower end with the seam of one leg at B and secure with two or three stitches. This anchors the pad in place while you stitch it. Finish off your thread and rejoin at the heel fold line which should be aligned with the back of the leg. Take a few stitches to hold it in place and then continue with backstitch round the foot pad. When complete, turn the legs right sides out, turning the top part first – the lower leg and foot will follow through.

5 *Preparing the head* As the head will be stuffed quite firmly use your thread double for sewing the head pieces together. Thread your needle and knot the ends together. Pin the two head pieces together with right sides facing and begin by sewing the seam from A (front neck) to B (nose). Work a double stitch at B but do not finish off the thread. (You will continue using this thread to attach the head gusset.)

6 *Attaching the head gusset* Beginning at the centre mark on the rounded end of the head gusset, sew the gusset to one head piece, starting at B (nose) and

TIP – Firm filling

Bear tweezers are invaluable for filling the bear's limbs because you can literally put the filling where you want it and get right to the tip of the paws and pads. These also enable you to pack the filling in which gives a good firm finish to your bear. For details of where to obtain bear tweezers see Suppliers, page 95.

ending at C (back neck). Finish off the thread. If there is any excess fabric at the end of the head gusset you must cut it off now. To complete the head start with a new double length of thread. Return to the centre of the nose and sew the head and head gusset from B back to C on the other side of the head. It's a good idea to work a tacking stitch (see pointers, page 11) at C to hold the pieces while sewing. When completed turn right sides out.

7 *Filling the head* Now it's time to fill the head. Do not fill the body or the limbs yet. Pull the filling apart and then insert small amounts at a time. Stuff the head firmly and in particular the nose area.

8 *Sculpting the eye sockets* Before inserting the eyes it is a good idea to sculpt the eye sockets so that the eyes fit well into the head rather than sitting on the front like frogs' eyes. Use two pins to locate the correct position of the eyes – they should be placed at the back of the nose, close to the head gusset seams. Make sure they are level. Pull out one of the pins slightly. Strengthen your thread with beeswax and double it. Insert your needle through the head

Actual-size pattern for Goldie

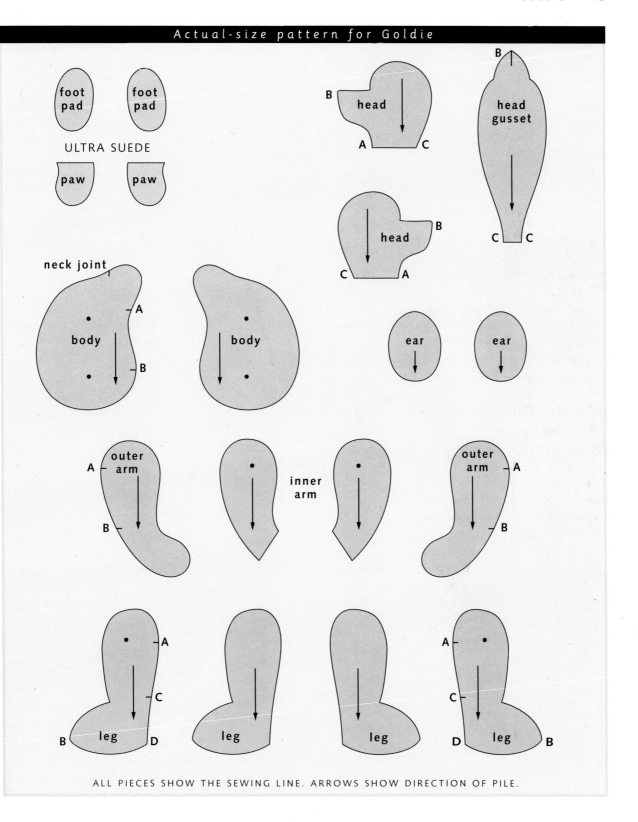

ALL PIECES SHOW THE SEWING LINE. ARROWS SHOW DIRECTION OF PILE.

opening and bring it out near the head. Take a small stitch (preferably across the head gusset seam) bringing the needle out at the head opening. Take another stitch in the same way close to the first stitch but not in the same holes. Remove the marker pin and pull the thread tight. Now sculpt the other eye socket in the same way using the

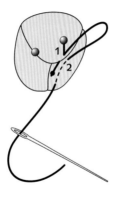

same thread. Tie a knot in the thread and use your needle to slip it down tight against the head. Bring the needle out on top of the head in the area where one of the ears will be attached and snip off the thread ends.

9 *Adding the eyes* Slip a bead onto a long length of black extra-strong nylon thread. Push both ends of the thread through the eye of a needle. Remove one of the pins marking the eye positions. Insert your needle into one

eye socket and bring it out at the head opening. Check that the eye is in the correct position. Slip off your needle and tie the two ends of thread together. Starting with a new length of thread repeat the process for the other eye. Tie

just one knot with the two sets of threads and then pull the threads very tightly so the eyes embed themselves in their sockets. Keep a firm tension on the threads and tie off securely with several knots. Cut off the thread ends.

10 *Preparing the head joint* Thread your needle with extra-strong nylon thread and knot both ends together to make a double thread. Work small running stitches around the head opening. Insert the

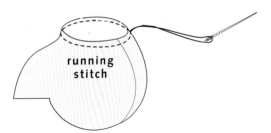

running stitch

round pin cotter pin joint with one washer placed on it and then pull the running stitch tight so the opening is completely closed with just the joint peg protruding. Secure the thread

and finish by working several extra stitches around the peg. Cut off the excess thread. It is most important that the opening is securely finished.

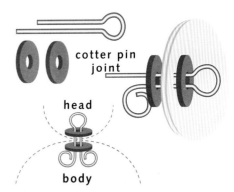

cotter pin joint

head

body

11 *Attaching the head* Insert the pin of the cotter pin joint through the body at the point indicated on the pattern. Through the body opening, peel the fabric back so the pin is accessible and put on the other washer. Open out the two prongs of the pin and curl each one round, back onto the washer, using either small short-nose pliers or a small cotter key. (For details of where to obtain a small cotter key see Suppliers, page 95.)

12 *Making the ears* Fold each ear in half lengthways with right sides together and stitch round the semi-circle, leaving the thread attached at the end. Cut along the fold and turn out. Ladder stitch along the opening. Fold in half again and stitch the two corners together, still leaving the thread attached. Pin the ears to the head in line with the head gusset seam and attach using ladder stitch. (See also an alternative method of attaching the ears, given right, which is equally effective.)

◆**13**◆ *Attaching the limbs* Put a washer on a cotter pin. Place a stiletto inside the limb and make a hole exactly where the joint position is marked. Then insert the cotter pin through the hole. Place a stiletto inside the body cavity and make a hole where the joint position is marked for the limb. Insert the cotter pin from the right side of the body through the hole into the body cavity and put on a washer. Open out the two prongs of the pin and curl each one round, back onto the washer inside the body cavity.

◆**14**◆ *Filling the bear* When all the limbs and head have been attached to the body you can fill the limbs and body. Be sure to put plenty of filling in the pads of the arms and also at the front of the feet. Do not over fill the limbs and body – they should not be as firm as the head. Then, using a double length of matching thread, close each seam with ladder stitch. (Run the thread over beeswax to give it extra strength – you will need to pull it up tightly so that your stitches disappear.)

◆**15**◆ *Adding the nose* It is easier to do the nose last because you can hold the bear better and also see how it looks. Each bear will be different – some may need a larger nose, some a smaller nose. Start by carefully clipping the pile away around the nose. Cut a tiny triangle of black ultra suede and use a dab of glue to stick it in place – this makes a good template for stitching the nose. Let the glue dry thoroughly. Using one strand of black stranded cotton and no knot, insert the needle at the back of the

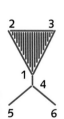

head and come out at 1. Do not pull right through – leave a short length which can be cut off once the nose is complete. Go in at 2 and back out at 3. Insert the needle back into 2, come out again at 3 and then go back in at 1. This gives you a small triangle. Fill it with close satin stitches, working over the outline, then bring your needle out at 1, ready to work the mouth.

Alternative method of attaching ears

Carrie Attwood of Littlebloomers (see page 95) shared this method with me, and I have found it to be a failsafe one.

✳ *Attaching the first ear* Run a length of matching thread through beeswax to strengthen it and knot the ends together. Insert the needle into one corner of the ear (1) and then into the head to the right of the right-hand eye where the lower end of the ear will go (2). Bring the needle out above the eye near the head gusset seam (3), insert the needle into the other corner of the ear (4) and then back into the head next to the point where you brought the needle out (5).

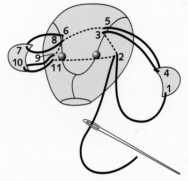

✳ *Attaching the second ear* Take the needle through the head of the bear and bring it out just above the left eye, where the top of the left ear will go (6). Insert the needle into the corner of the other ear (7) and go back into the head close to the point where you brought the needle out (8). Bring the needle out level with the bottom of the other ear but on the left-hand side of the bear (9) and pass it through the second corner of the second ear (10). Finally, insert the needle close to where you brought it out of the head (11) and pass it right through the bear's head, coming out at your original starting point. Pull the thread tightly. If you wish to make any slight adjustments you can do this by taking a few extra stitches. (Use waxed dental floss for attaching ears as the stitching will not be seen.)

✳ *Strengthening the ears* Secure by bringing your needle out at the centre back of one ear, passing the needle through the ear to the front of the head and taking a tiny stitch in the head. Pass the needle back into the ear and then into the head at the back and pull tightly. Work extra stitches if they are needed. Repeat for the other ear. To finish your thread tie a knot, run it down to the fabric and 'pop' it through the bear's head.

16 *Working the mouth* Take the needle down at position 4 and out at 5. Now take the needle through the loop made at position 4 and back in at 6 to give the other side of the mouth. Finally, bring your needle out at the back of the head, take a tiny stitch and bring your needle out somewhere away from the stitch. Cut off the black thread very close to the fabric and the end should disappear.

17 *Finishing your bear* Brush your bear gently with a small teasel brush, paying particular attention to the seams, then add a bow using one of the two methods given right. If you have narrow ribbon, make a basic bow, but with wide ribbon follow the instructions for a pinched bow.

The bear shown here has been adapted to commemorate a golden wedding anniversary. Highlight the nose using a single strand of gold metallic embroidery thread (I used Madeira machine embroidery thread), working a few stitches across the width of the nose. Then add a bow made from gold ribbon and if you wish embellish it further by adding tiny gold beads or French knots to the ribbon or even the bear.

Making bows

BASIC BOW The secret of a good bow is to start with a length of ribbon approximately 8-10in (20-25cm) long. Put the ribbon round the bear's neck with an equal length on each side. Pass the left end over the right end and back under. Make a loop with the left end, take the right end round behind the loop previously made, over your left second finger in an anti-clockwise direction. With your left thumb push the ribbon through the loop made by your finger. Carefully pull the two loops to form a bow which will have both the ribbon ends pointing downwards.

PINCHED BOW This is used if the ribbon is too wide to go round the bear's neck. Thread a needle with the same colour thread as the ribbon and knot the ends together. Take a 6in (15cm) length of ribbon and loop the ends to form a bow shape. Take your threaded needle round the cross-over point several times and pull tight. Secure well and leave the needle and thread attached. Position the bow on the bear's neck, then wrap the thread round the neck. Finish the thread by sewing into the centre of the bow. Trim off the thread ends.

FINISHING RIBBON BOWS To prevent the ribbon fraying fold each end in half lengthways and use very sharp scissors to cut across the ribbon at a slant, pointing down towards the fold. When opened out, the end of the ribbon will have a V-shape. Alternatively, do not fold the ribbon but just trim the ends diagonally, as shown.

ANNIVERSARY BEARS

Bears make wonderful presents that rarely fail to please, and because the miniature bears in this book are so small there will always be a space for them in any home. In particular, because they are associated with love, bears make superb wedding anniversary presents. All you need to do is make a few slight adjustments or add appropriate trimmings to link your bear with the wedding anniversary in question.

Set the mood for your anniversary bear with the fabric. For example, to commemorate a ruby wedding anniversary make your bear out of a piece of ruby-coloured fabric. Ruby ribbon would probably look too drab so try using a paler ribbon and add burgundy seed beads or embroider the ribbon with burgundy French knots before tying it round the bear's neck.

Here are some more ideas.

1st: paper Give the bear some origami to hold and add other pieces round his feet.

2nd: cotton Sit the bear on a cotton reel.

3rd: leather Make a bear with leather paws and pads.

4th: fruit Sit the bear next to a fruit basket and give him some fruit to hold made from Fimo or modelling clay.

5th: wood You could set your bear up as a castaway on a wooden raft or simply glue a twig to one paw, perhaps decorated with tiny cake decorators' flowers so it looks like a flowering branch – a gift of peace.

6th: sugar Give the bear with a box of sweets.

7th: wool Make your bear a sweater, like the one given for the skier on page 68 or knit him a simple scarf. Alternatively, give him some small balls of wool to hold and place others around him.

8th: bronze Sit the bear on a bronze coin.

9th: pottery Dolls' house pots could be useful here if you get your bear to hold one. Alternatively, buy a full-size pot and simply sit your bear inside it.

10th: tin Cut a star or heart from tin foil and stick it on your bear's chest, then trim him with a silver ribbon too, or thread a tin-coloured trinket on a ribbon around his neck.

11th: steel Give your bear a necklace of shiny metallic beads, for example.

12th: silk Simply tie a silk ribbon round the bear's neck.

13th: lace Put a little lace ruff around the neck of the bear by working running stitch along one edge of an 8in (20cm) length of lace ribbon and then gathering it up to fit round the neck. Secure to the back of the bear's neck with a double stitch. If you like add a little ribbon on the head to make this into a girl bear.

14th: ivory Fake ivory will do here. Give your bear an ivory-look button to hold, for example.

15th: crystal Make a necklace of glass beads to hang round the bear's neck.

16th: china Buy a china item, such as a vase, from a dolls' house supplier for the bear to hold. Alternatively, buy a pretty loving cup or mug and pop your bear inside it.

25th: silver Make a silver ribbon bow to go round the bear's neck or even make the bear from silver fabric.

30th: pearl Pop a pearl pendant round the bear's neck and sit him next to an oyster shell.

35th: coral Add a necklace of coral beads to link your bear with the theme or make the bear in coral-coloured fabric.

40th: ruby Make a ruby red bear or give a bear a dolls' house bottle of ruby wine to hold.

45th: sapphire Make your bear in blue fabric and give him an appropriate ribbon such as silver ribbon decorated with blue French knots or blue beads. Highlight the bear's nose with blue metallic thread.

50th: gold Put a small gold ring on a ribbon round the bear's neck or make a cream bear and trim with golden ribbon. Work the bear's nose in brown and highlight with gold thread.

55th: emerald Try making a green bear or make an ordinary brown bear and give him a large green bow.

60th: diamond Find a lovely cut glass or crystal bead and thread it on a length of embroidery thread or fine ribbon to go round the neck of the bear – it will look really special.

RUSSELL AND ROSIE

The teddy has been called the world's most popular soft toy and in Britain 63 out of every 100 homes have one.

A good way of giving a bear a smart new look is to make the head and paws from one fabric and the rest of him or her from another fabric. This makes the bear look as if it is wearing a suit with matching shoes. Try experimenting with different selections of fabric and you'll find your bear takes on a new look each time. Here, the same pattern was used to make a boy bear, Russell, and his sister, Rosie. Russell has a dark gold head and paws and his body is clad in navy-blue spotted fabric while Rosie is made from light pink rayon fabric with her body in burgundy spotted upholstery fabric.

Notice that the bears have contrasting noses for additional character and are wearing animal slippers for a humorous touch. These are added simply by stitching small ears to the tops of the feet, with tiny beads for the eyes and an embroidered nose. These bears look very dressy – perfect for a special occasion.

You will need

- ⊹ 4 x 4in (10 x 10cm) square of miniature bear upholstery fabric for the head and outer paws
- ⊹ 6 x 4in (15 x 10cm) piece of miniature bear upholstery fabric for the body and limbs
- ⊹ Small piece of contrasting miniature bear upholstery fabric for the nose
- ⊹ Ultra suede for paws (similar colour to nose fabric)
- ⊹ Ultra suede for the foot pads to match body fabric
- ⊹ General-purpose sewing thread to match main fabrics
- ⊹ Extra-strong black nylon thread
- ⊹ Black stranded embroidery thread for the nose
- ⊹ Black ultra suede for the nose
- ⊹ Darning and fine sharp needles
- ⊹ Polyester filling
- ⊹ Pair of tiny (2mm) matching black beads or bear eyes
- ⊹ Four ¼in (6mm) 'T' pin fibreboard cotter pin joints
- ⊹ One ¼in (6mm) round pin fibreboard cotter pin joint

- ⊹ Small teasel brush
- ⊹ Stiletto

For trimming Russell
- ⊹ Light blue ultra suede or fine felt
- ⊹ Four matching white/pearl seed beads for rabbits' eyes
- ⊹ Narrow white braid
- ⊹ Light blue silk ribbon
- ⊹ Three small buttons
- ⊹ Pink embroidery thread for the rabbits' noses
- ⊹ Nylon monofil thread (invisible thread)

For trimming Rosie
- ⊹ Pink ultra suede or fine felt
- ⊹ Four matching white/pearl seed beads for mice's eyes
- ⊹ Narrow white braid
- ⊹ 9in (23cm) length of narrow pink or white lace
- ⊹ Three pearl beads for buttons
- ⊹ Pink embroidery thread for the mice's noses
- ⊹ Nylon monofil thread (invisible thread)

Making Russell

Trace the pattern pieces for Russell from page 23 and use them to make card templates (see page 9). Transfer the inner paws and pads onto a single layer of ultra suede and cut out, adding an ⅛in (3mm) seam allowance around each piece. Transfer the front head, back head, ear and outer paw onto the wrong side of a single layer of the face fabric with the arrow on the pattern pointing in the direction of the fabric pile. Then transfer the nose onto contrasting fabric and the remaining pieces onto the body fabric in the same way. Make sure you transfer the joint position marks onto the two body pieces and the appropriate arms and legs – this is most important. Cut out the pieces, adding an ⅛in (3mm) seam allowance around each one. Make the bear following the instructions below, using backstitch for seams and ladder stitch for closing seams (see page 10).

1 *Starting the bear* With right sides facing backstitch the body pieces together and make the arms and legs in the same way as for Goldie, steps 1-4 (pages 13-14). Note that the outer arms have an outer paw. With right sides facing, sew the straight edge of an outer paw to the straight edge of each outer arm before joining the two main arm pieces together.

2 *Starting the head* The head is constructed quite differently from Goldie's head. Place both back head pieces together with right sides facing and stitch from A to B using a double thread. Set this piece to one side. Now put one front head and one nose piece together with right sides facing and stitch the curve from C to D, easing the pieces as you go – you'll find it helps if you let the pieces curve in your hand while you stitch. Repeat with the other front head and nose. Now put the right sides together of the pieces you have just sewn and use thread to match the nose to sew round the nose from C to D. Finish off the thread at D. Using thread to match the main head fabric sew from C to E. Also sew from D to F. Take the joined back head and with right sides together position A on the back head to E on the front head. Stitch from AE to G. Return to AE and sew from AE to H.

3 *Sculpting the eyes* Turn the head right sides out and stuff it. Mark the position of the eyes with glass-headed pins. The eyes should be positioned between the contrasting fabric and the back of the head seam. Now thread sculpt the eye sockets with a double length of matching waxed thread in the same way as for Goldie, page 14, step 8.

4 *Completing the bear* Add the eyes, prepare and attach the head, then add the ears and limbs before stuffing the bear and stitching the nose and mouth (see steps 9-16 for Goldie on pages 14-18). Finally, brush up the fur with a small teasel brush.

Trimming Russell

1 *Trimming the wrists* Using a double length of nylon invisible thread stitch a length of braid round each arm where the paws join the body fabric.

2 *Making the slippers* Using a double length of nylon invisible thread sew two seed beads for eyes onto the front of each foot. Then, using one strand of pink embroidery thread work a tiny nose in satin stitch. Using

the pattern on page 23 cut out the rabbit ears in either ultra suede or fine felt – there is no need to add a seam allowance. Pinch together the base of one of the ears and use a double length of nylon invisible thread to stitch it in place on the foot. Repeat to stitch another ear in place on the same foot, then attach two ears to the other foot in the same way, making sure they look well balanced.

3 *Completing the trimmings* Tie a bow round Russell's neck with the blue silk ribbon (see page 18) and then sew three small buttons down the front of the body to complete the look.

Making and trimming Rosie

1 *Making the bear* Make Rosie in exactly the same way as her brother and using the same pattern but in pink or red fabrics instead of blue ones. Then use a double length of nylon invisible thread to stitch a length of braid round each arm where the paws join the body fabric.

2 *Trimming Rosie* The mice on Rosie's slippers are added in the same way as the rabbits on the boy's slippers (see step 2, left) but instead of using rabbit ears cut

Presenting your bear

If your bear is intended as a gift it is nice to present it in a hand-finished box or tin so that it can be kept safely as long as needed. As it is a very personal gift it makes a nice touch to line the box or tin in a luxury fabric such as silk. Only a small piece is required and you can often find inexpensive remnants at fabric suppliers or buy them from shops which make wedding gowns. You will need a piece of fabric approximately 3in (8cm) longer and wider than the box base. To line a small box or tin first stick a strip of double-sided tape around the inside edge of the base. Remove the protective backing from the tape and position the fabric in the box. Turning the edges of the fabric under, carefully stick them to the tape, gathering the fabric as you go. Then simply lay your bear in splendour on top.

FINISHED SIZE
2½IN (6.5CM)

the mouse ears from the pattern below (without adding a seam allowance). Attach them to the slippers in the same way as the rabbit ears, then complete the slippers in the same way as Russell's. Work a line of running stitch along one edge of a 9in (23cm) length of white or pink lace and

pull up the thread to gather it. Fit it round Rosie's neck and knot the gathering thread at the back. Trim off the thread end. Finally, sew three small pearl beads down the front of Rosie's body and give that finishing touch by tying a tiny bow to stitch on her head.

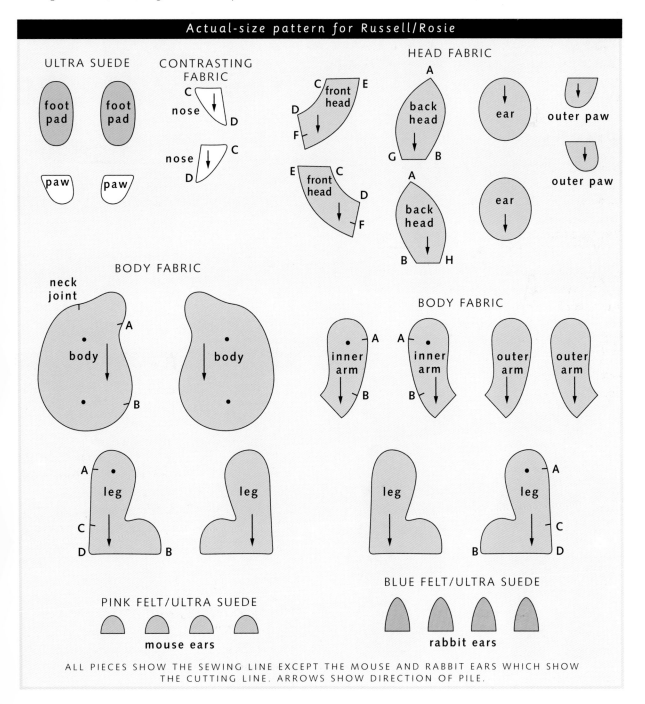

Actual-size pattern for Russell/Rosie

ULTRA SUEDE

CONTRASTING FABRIC

HEAD FABRIC

foot pad   foot pad

nose

back head

ear

outer paw

paw   paw

nose

front head

back head

ear

outer paw

BODY FABRIC

neck joint

body   body

BODY FABRIC

inner arm   inner arm   outer arm   outer arm

leg   leg   leg   leg

PINK FELT/ULTRA SUEDE

mouse ears

BLUE FELT/ULTRA SUEDE

rabbit ears

ALL PIECES SHOW THE SEWING LINE EXCEPT THE MOUSE AND RABBIT EARS WHICH SHOW THE CUTTING LINE. ARROWS SHOW DIRECTION OF PILE.

WILLIAM

Teddies may have originated in Germany – at the same time that Morris Michtom was making bears in the USA, Richard Steiff made a fully jointed bear for the 1903 Leipzig Toy Fair in Germany. Today Steiff is still one of the top bear manufacturers.

William has just graduated from bear school and would make the perfect gift for another graduate or for any adult or child who has just passed an exam – his gown and mortarboard can easily be personalised to suit the recipient. William stands 3½in (9cm) tall and is made from a wonderful bright gold upholstery fabric with matching paws and pads. His body has darts at top and bottom to give him a fatter tummy and his limbs are thread-jointed.

FINISHED SIZE
3½IN (9CM)

You will need

- ✢ 6 x 9in (15 x 23cm) piece of bright gold miniature bear upholstery fabric
- ✢ Matching ultra suede for paws and pads
- ✢ General-purpose sewing thread to match main fabric
- ✢ Extra-strong black nylon thread
- ✢ Black stranded embroidery thread for the nose
- ✢ Black ultra suede for the nose
- ✢ Darning and fine sharp needles
- ✢ Polyester filling
- ✢ Pair of tiny (2mm) matching black beads or bear eyes
- ✢ One ¼in (6mm) round pin fibreboard cotter pin joint
- ✢ Small teasel brush
- ✢ Extra-strong brown nylon thread for jointing

For dressing William
- ✢ Black cotton fabric
- ✢ Black felt
- ✢ Approximately 7in (18cm) of narrow (2mm wide) gold silk ribbon
- ✢ Scrap of Bondaweb (fusible bonding fabric)
- ✢ Gold embroidery thread
- ✢ Scrap of cream-coloured paper for the scroll
- ✢ 1in (2.5cm) diameter marble for a mould
- ✢ Cling film
- ✢ Fabric stiffener or solution of 50:50 PVA glue/water
- ✢ Fabric glue

Making William

Trace the pattern pieces for William from page 26 and use them to make card templates (see page 9). Transfer the paws and pads onto a single layer of ultra suede and cut out, adding an ⅛in (3mm) seam allowance around each piece. Transfer the remaining pieces onto the wrong side of a single layer of bright gold miniature bear upholstery fabric with the arrow on the pattern pointing in the direction of the fabric pile. Cut out the pieces, adding an ⅛in (3mm) seam allowance around each one. Make the bear following the instructions below, using backstitch for seams and ladder stitch for closing seams (see page 10).

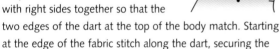

1 *Stitching the darts* Take one body piece and fold it in half with right sides together so that the two edges of the dart at the top of the body match. Starting at the edge of the fabric stitch along the dart, securing the

thread well at the end. Turn the fabric over and check that the dart has created a pointed shape. Stitch the bottom dart in the same way and then stitch the two darts on the other body piece.

2 *Joining the main pieces* Assemble the bear in the same way as Goldie, steps 1-12, pages 13-17, joining the body pieces and making the head. As the limbs are to be thread-jointed fill the limbs at the same time as you fill the head, putting plenty of filling into the pads of the arms and the front of the feet. Stuff each limb firmly. Run matching thread over beeswax to give it extra strength. Then, using a double length of thread, close each seam in the limbs with ladder stitch. Once the head has been attached stuff the body, but not as firmly as the head, then close the gap in the seam with ladder stitch in the same way as for the limbs. Add the eyes and make and attach the ears.

3 *Positioning the limbs* Use four pins to mark the positions of the arms and legs. Make sure the tops of the arms are level and are positioned more towards the

back of the body than the front. The legs should line up directly under the arm positions and should be approximately ½in (12mm) up from the bottom of the body. Check the tops of the bear's legs are level and that he will be able to stand up straight and sit correctly.

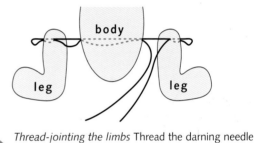

4 *Thread-jointing the limbs* Thread the darning needle with approximately 20in (51cm) of extra-strong nylon thread and knot both ends together to make a double thread. With the bear facing you, insert the needle into the right-hand side of the body at one leg pin and bring it out on the other side where the other pin is. Do not pull all the thread through. Pass the needle through the left leg then pass it back through the leg, making sure it goes back into the same hole it came out of – otherwise your bear will have a dimple when the thread is pulled tight. Check the thread is free running and that you have not caught the original thread on your return journey, then bring it out again at the right-hand side of the body. Pass the needle through the right leg and back the same way to bring it out between the right leg and the body; tie one knot and pull very tightly. Check the legs are correctly positioned and then secure with several knots. Cut off the knot on the very end of the thread and take each end back into the body before cutting off. Thread joint the arms in the same way.

5 *Completing the bear* Work the bear's nose and mouth in the same way as for Goldie, steps 15-16 on pages 17-18, then give him a brush with a teasel brush, concentrating on the seams. To add claws, see page 46.

Dressing William

1 *Preparing the gown* Trace the patterns for William's gown and yoke from page 27. Cut the gown from black cotton fabric, folding the fabric in half first and placing the pattern on the fold as indicated. Cut the yoke from unfolded fabric. Do not add seam allowances. Turn under 1/8in (3mm) along the long straight edge of the gown and stitch in place; press well. Using black thread work tiny running stitch along the neatened edge and pull up into a gentle gather.

2 *Attaching the yoke* Place the two yoke pieces together with right sides facing and stitch from A round the edge to B. Turn out, close seam with ladder stitch, and press. Lay the yoke over the gown with right sides facing, matching the pieces at C on both ends and secure with a small stitch, if required. Ease the gathers on the gown to fit round the outer edge of the yoke and stitch the two pieces together. Backstitch from E to F to join the side seams; hem the sleeves.

3 *Completing the gown* The front and neck edge of the gown is trimmed with gold silk ribbon which is attached with Bondaweb. Cut short strips of Bondaweb which are narrower than the ribbon. Starting at the hem of one front edge of the gown turn the raw edge of the ribbon under and then lay a strip of Bondaweb on the gown. Lay the ribbon over it and use the point of the iron to press and fuse the ribbon in place. Continue with another strip of Bondaweb and ribbon until you reach the top. Here turn the ribbon back on itself to go round the neck and continue on down to the hem on the other front. Fit the gown on the bear and secure with a few stitches.

Actual-size pattern for William

ALL PIECES SHOW THE SEWING LINE. ARROWS SHOW DIRECTION OF PILE.

4 *Shaping the mortarboard* Cut a 1¼in (3m) square of black felt and a 1in (2.5cm) circle of black felt (a £2 coin makes a good template) and soak both pieces in fabric stiffener or glue solution. Leave the square to dry. Cover the marble with cling film and press the damp circle of felt on top. Layer another piece of cling film over the top and smooth the felt down over the marble. Leave for ten minutes then remove the cling film and leave to dry for 2-3 hours.

5 *Completing the mortarboard* When both pieces of felt are completely dry, trim the edges neatly if required and then glue the round piece to the centre of the square. Cut four lengths of gold thread 4½in (11.5cm) long and tie a knot with all four lengths. Ask someone to hold the knotted end while you twist the other end until the cord starts to wrinkle, then take hold of both ends and fold in half. Give the cord a shake to make it lie flat then knot the two ends together. Glue the cord and tassel to the centre of one edge of the mortarboard, then fit the mortarboard on the bear's head (see the photograph right).

6 *Making the scroll* Make a scroll by rolling up a 1in (2.5cm) square of cream paper and tie in place with a piece of gold embroidery thread. Stitch the scroll to the bear's paw.

Actual-size pattern for William's gown

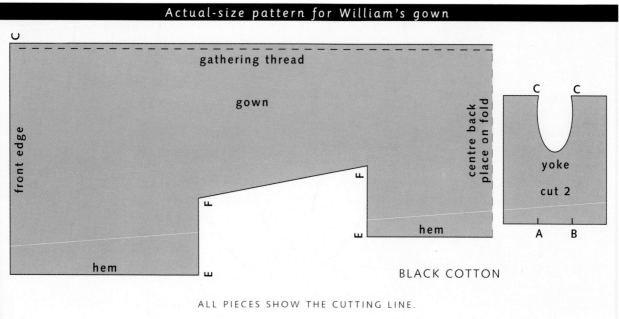

gathering thread

gown

front edge

centre back
place on fold

C   C

yoke

cut 2

A   B

hem

hem

BLACK COTTON

ALL PIECES SHOW THE CUTTING LINE.

CHICO THE CLOWN

'Whoever said "diamonds are a girl's best friend" would retract that statement after seeing the sparkle in a teddy's eyes.'

LANA T. ZEIS

Meet Chico. With his round red nose, large, innocent eyes and colourful ultra suede hands and feet he already looks like a clown even before you add his costume and hat. He's a fun bear to make with plenty of scope for fancy trimmings and his head is constructed differently with a 'pop-on' nose which enables you to use another fabric.

Since the bear is dressed in full costume his body isn't visible so it does not really matter what fabric you use to make him. However, I chose white fabric so that it would not show through his pale clothes or give a shadow under them. (If you prefer you can use the same colour for the head and body of the bear.) I also used a scrap of red long-pile fabric for the back of his head which looks like his hair. As the final touch I gave the bear a toy trumpet and flower to hold. A small trumpet like this is available from dolls' house suppliers and there are instructions for making the flower.

You will need

- ✤ 6 x 9in (15 x 23cm) piece of miniature bear fabric for the body (American upholstery fabric, short-pile mohair or soft upholstery fabric)
- ✤ 3^1/$_8$ x 3^1/$_2$in (8 x 9cm) square of bear-coloured miniature bear fabric (optional) for the head
- ✤ 1in (2.5cm) square of red miniature bear fabric for nose
- ✤ 1^1/$_2$in (4cm) square of red ^{5}/$_8$in (1.5cm) long pile fabric for the back of the head (optional)
- ✤ Small pieces of yellow and green ultra suede for the hands and feet
- ✤ Small piece of white ultra suede for the eye patch
- ✤ General-purpose sewing thread in red, white and to match the main fabric
- ✤ Extra-strong black nylon thread
- ✤ Extra-strong red nylon thread
- ✤ Black stranded embroidery thread for the nose
- ✤ Metallic thread to highlight the nose
- ✤ Darning and fine sharp needles

- ✤ Polyester filling
- ✤ Pair of ^{1}/$_8$in (3mm) matching black beads or bear eyes
- ✤ Four ^{1}/$_4$in (6mm) 'T' pin fibreboard cotter pin joints
- ✤ One ^{1}/$_4$in (6mm) round pin fibreboard cotton pin joint
- ✤ Stiletto
- ✤ Small teasel brush

For trimming Chico

- ✤ Fabric and matching thread for the suit
- ✤ About 12in (30cm) of red mohair knitting wool or tiny red pompons
- ✤ Red cotton perlé
- ✤ Small piece of white felt for the hat
- ✤ Nylon monofil thread (invisible thread)
- ✤ 12in (30cm) of yellow satin ribbon ^{3}/$_4$in (1.5cm) wide
- ✤ Small pieces of brightly coloured ultra suede for his flower
- ✤ A green pipe cleaner for the flower stalk

Making Chico

Trace the pattern pieces for Chico from page 30 and use them to make card templates (see page 9). Transfer the feet, hands, pads and eye patch onto a single layer of ultra suede and cut out, adding an ¹⁄₈in (3mm) seam allowance around each piece. Note the colours each piece should be cut from. Transfer one head and the ears onto the wrong side of a single layer of your bear-coloured fabric with the arrow on the pattern pointing in the direction of the fabric pile. Transfer the other head onto red long-pile fabric for the hair, or use your bear-coloured fabric if you prefer. Transfer the nose onto red upholstery fabric and the remaining pieces onto your body fabric in the same way. Make sure you transfer the joint position marks onto the two body pieces and the appropriate arms and legs – this is most important. Cut out the pieces, adding an ¹⁄₈in (3mm) seam allowance around each one. Make the bear following the instructions below, using backstitch for seams and ladder stitch for closing seams (see page 10).

1 *Getting started* Join the body pieces in the same way as for Goldie, step 1 (page 13). With right sides together, sew the straight edge of one yellow hand to the straight edge of one inner arm, taking an ¹⁄₈in (3mm) seam allowance. Then sew the straight edge of the other yellow hand to the straight edge of one outer arm. Repeat for green hands. Then, with right sides together, sew each inner arm to an outer arm, beginning at A and working round the top, side and lower edge to B. Turn right sides out, turning the top part first – the hand will follow through.

2 *Sewing the legs* Matching A and B in each case, stitch the straight edge of a foot to the straight edge of a leg. Both the yellow feet should point in one direction and the green feet in the opposite direction. Pin a leg with a green foot to a leg with a yellow foot with right sides facing and stitch together from A at the back ankle up to D at the leg opening. Then stitch from C to B and on to E at the front of the shoe. Leave the thread attached. Repeat to stitch the other leg. Turn the legs right side out. Anchor the foot pad at the back of the foot with a tiny stitch. Using the thread which is still attached at the front

FINISHED SIZE
4IN (10CM)

of the shoe, attach the front end of the foot pad and continue stitching all round the pad with small running stitch. Repeat for the other leg.

3 *Stitching the head* Pin the two head pieces together with right sides facing and use a double length of matching thread to backstitch from A to B, leaving the straight edge open. Turn right sides out. Stuff firmly, moulding the head into a round ball. Gently brush the seam with a teasel brush. Pin the eye patch on the face and use white thread and ladder stitch to secure it around the top curved edge (the lower edge will be secured by the nose).

Now use black embroidery cotton to add a single stitch up the centre of each eye. Work the eyebrows with two joining arches in backstitch, using the photograph as a guide. Tie off the ends of the thread through the head opening.

Actual-size pattern for Chico the Clown

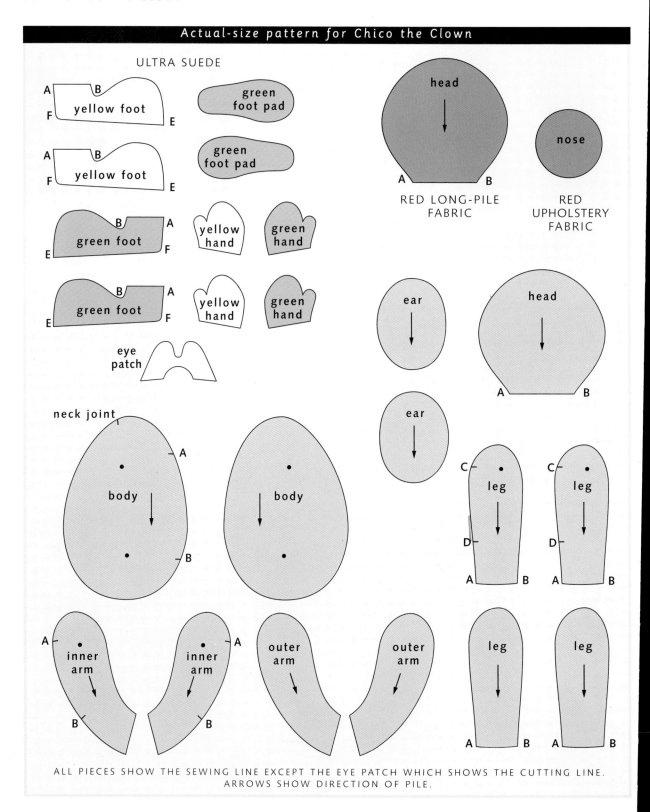

ULTRA SUEDE

yellow foot

green foot pad

yellow foot

green foot pad

green foot

yellow hand

green hand

green foot

yellow hand

green hand

eye patch

neck joint

body

body

inner arm

inner arm

outer arm

outer arm

head

nose

RED LONG-PILE FABRIC

RED UPHOLSTERY FABRIC

ear

head

ear

leg

leg

leg

leg

ALL PIECES SHOW THE SEWING LINE EXCEPT THE EYE PATCH WHICH SHOWS THE CUTTING LINE. ARROWS SHOW DIRECTION OF PILE.

4 *Adding the nose* Using strong red nylon thread with a knot in the end work a small running stitch around the nose approximately ⅛in (3mm) from the edge. Gently pull the thread to gather in the sides and insert a small amount of stuffing. Pull the thread tight and secure well, but do not cut the needle and thread off. You should now have a small ball which is ready to be attached to the head. Pin the nose on the head with the gathered side towards the head. The nose should be positioned not quite in the centre but slightly lower as shown in the photograph. Ladder stitch the nose in position using the red nylon thread which is still attached. Pull the stitches tight so the nose blends in and looks part of the head, not just stuck on as an afterthought.

5 *Completing the bear* Complete the bear following steps 8-17 for Goldie (pages 14-18). When you come to work the nose, highlight it with metallic thread. There is no head gusset to use as a guide to locating the ears so place them on the head seam where they look right. For claws, see page 46.

Dressing and trimming Chico

1 *Cutting out the pieces* Trace the patterns for the clown's clothes and hat given on page 32. Cut out the hat from white felt then cut the remaining pieces from your chosen fabric.

2 *Making the suit* Fold the body of the suit with right sides facing so the two adjacent seams AB match. Stitch these seams taking an ⅛in (3mm) seam allowance. Now turn to the sleeves. To neaten the wrist edge on the sleeves turn 1/8in (3mm) to the wrong side along the long straight edge and press the fold firmly with your finger and thumb. Fold each sleeve in half to match the short straight edges and stitch this seam from C to D, then turn each sleeve right side out. Work a small running stitch around the top of the sleeve between E and F but do not finish off the thread. Insert one sleeve into the suit by matching the side seam and the sleeve seam. Pull up the running stitch and ease the top of the sleeve to fit into the armhole, securing the running stitch to hold the gathers in

place. Backstitch the seam. Repeat with the other sleeve. To shape the legs cut from G to H. Then, with right sides facing join the leg seams by stitching from G to H and also from I to J.

3 *Fitting the suit* Fit the suit on the bear with the opening at the back, then tuck in the seam allowances and stitch the centre back seam from H/I to K with ladder stitch. Now use a double length of matching thread to work running stitch around each cuff where you folded the unfinished edge under. Do not finish off the thread but pull it up to gather the fabric tightly around the bear's wrists. Secure the thread and trim off the end. To make the pompons use red mohair knitting wool to work three two-turn French knots (see page 10) down the centre of the suit. Use the photograph as a guide.

4 *Making the hat* Fold the hat to match the straight edges and ladder stitch the seam from A to B using nylon monofil invisible thread. Now use one strand of red cotton perlé to work a decorative oversewing stitch all round the bottom of the hat. Turn a small brim over and stitch in place. Using red cotton perlé work three two-turn French knots down the front of the hat, referring to the photograph as a guide to positioning. Fit the hat on the bear and use nylon monofil invisible thread to stitch it in place.

5 *Completing the outfit* Work a line of running stitch along one edge of an 8in (20cm) length of ribbon with each stitch approximately ¼in (6mm) long. Gently pull up the stitches to gather the ribbon and wrap it around Chico's neck. Secure the gathering and cut off the thread end. Now use red mohair knitting wool to tie two knots, one on top of the other. Cut off and use invisible nylon thread to sew the knots onto the top of one shoe. Repeat for the other shoe.

6 *Making the flower* Finally, make a flower using several colours of ultra suede. Using the pattern below cut out six petals and two centre circles – there is no need to add a seam allowance. I cut two petals from each of three colours and the centre from a fourth colour. Attach the petals to one of the circles and then place the other circle on top, covering the ends of the petals. Stitch in place with one tiny stitch. To make the flower stem cut a 2in (5cm) length of green pipe cleaner and trim back all the pile. Stitch it securely to the back of the flower using monofil invisible nylon thread, then stitch the flower to the bear's paw.

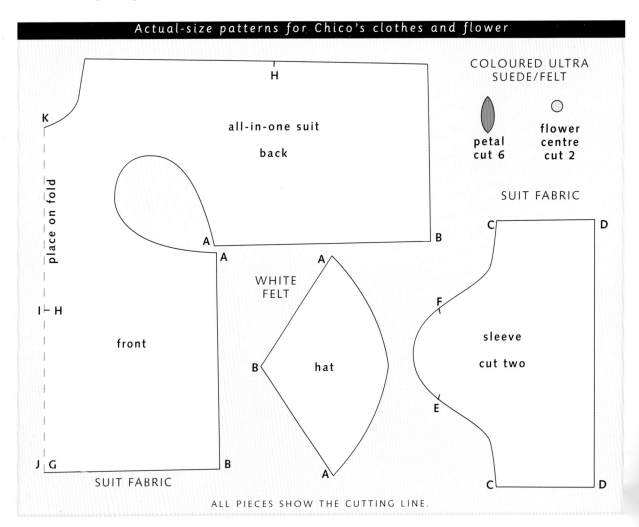

Actual-size patterns for Chico's clothes and flower

place on fold

all-in-one suit
back

COLOURED ULTRA
SUEDE/FELT

petal
cut 6

flower
centre
cut 2

SUIT FABRIC

WHITE
FELT

front

hat

sleeve
cut two

SUIT FABRIC

ALL PIECES SHOW THE CUTTING LINE.

ALFRED

There are more than 140 million teddy bears in the USA.

This benevolent bear is happy to spend his days resting in the comfort of a chair. He is designed as an older bear – his legs are bent and his arms fold over, perfectly fitting the contours of his rocker. Alfred is a retired bear now, and happy to sit and watch the world go by, making all who see him feel similarly relaxed.

Alfred was created by mother and daughter Wendy and Megan Chamberlain of Essential Bears in South Africa (see page 95). Megan started making medium to large bears but with the demand for smaller bears increasing she now makes mainly miniatures – usually one-of-a-kind bears or limited editions. Wendy and Megan hold regular workshops in their studio. Their award-winning bears are well known throughout South Africa and are now sold all over the world.

Making Alfred

Trace the pieces for Alfred from page 34 and use them to make card templates (see page 9). Transfer the foot pads onto a single layer of ultra suede and cut out, adding an ⅛in (3mm) seam allowance around each piece. Transfer the remaining bear pieces onto the wrong side of a single layer of miniature bear fabric with the arrow on the pattern pointing in the direction of the fabric pile. Cut out the pieces, adding an ⅛in (3mm) seam allowance around each one. Alfred is thread-jointed. Make the bear following the instructions below, using backstitch for joining pieces and ladder stitch for closing seams (see page 10).

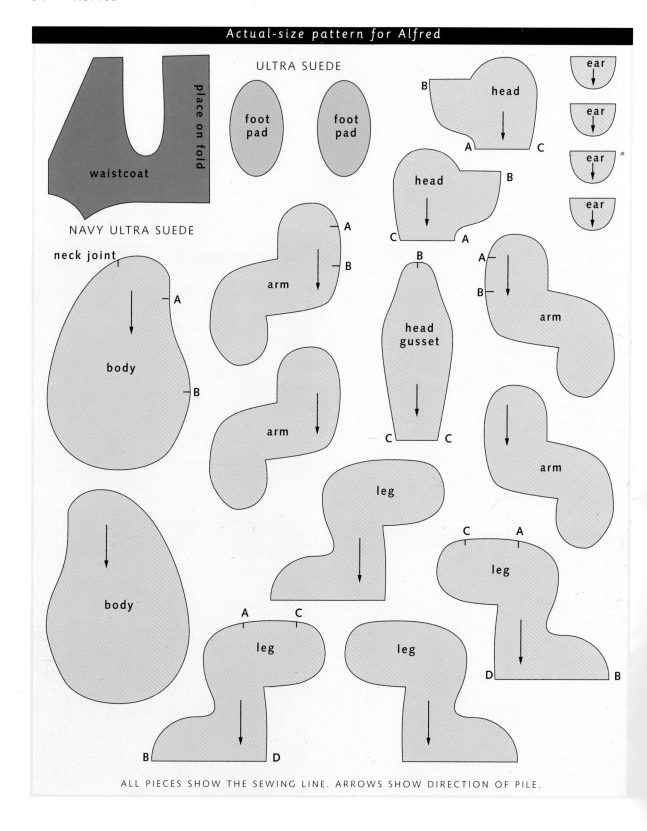

Actual-size pattern for Alfred

place on fold

waistcoat

ULTRA SUEDE

foot pad

foot pad

NAVY ULTRA SUEDE

neck joint

body

A

B

arm

A

B

arm

head gusset

B

C   C

head

B

A   C

head

B

C   A

ear

ear

ear

ear

A

B

arm

arm

leg

body

leg

A   C

leg

B   D

leg

C   A

leg

D   B

ALL PIECES SHOW THE SEWING LINE. ARROWS SHOW DIRECTION OF PILE.

You will need

+ 6 x 9in (15 x 23cm) piece of bright gold miniature bear fabric (American upholstery fabric, short-pile mohair or soft upholstery fabric)
+ Matching or toning ultra suede for foot pads
+ General-purpose sewing thread to match bear fabric
+ Black extra-strong nylon thread for attaching eyes
+ Black stranded embroidery thread for the nose
+ Black ultra suede for the nose
+ Darning and fine sharp needles
+ Polyester filling
+ Pair of tiny (2mm) black onyx beads for eyes
+ One ⅜in (10mm) fibreboard cotter pin joint for the neck
+ Stiletto
+ Small teasel brush
+ Extra-strong brown nylon thread for jointing

For dressing Alfred
+ Navy blue lightweight ultra suede for the waistcoat
+ Small piece of red lightweight ultra suede
+ Two ¼in (4mm) red buttons
+ Brown Fimo or modelling clay (optional)

1 *Making the body* Place the two body pieces together with right sides facing. Beginning at A with a double stitch, sew right round to B, being sure to stitch exactly on the pen line. Work a double stitch to finish, then knot the thread on the wrong side and trim off the thread end. Turn right sides out.

2 *Making the arms and legs* Pin the arm pieces together in pairs with right sides facing and raw edges matching. Stitch together, beginning at A and working round the top, side and lower edge to B. Turn right sides out, turning the top part first – the paw will follow through. The legs are a different shape from Goldie's but you make them in the same way, following steps 3-4 on pages 13-14.

3 *Preparing the pieces* Continue making the bear following steps 5-11 for Goldie (see pages 14-16). Fill the limbs at the same time as you fill the head, putting plenty of filling into the pads of the arms and the front of the feet. Add the eyes in the same way as for Goldie. Run matching thread over beeswax to give it extra

strength and then, using it double, close each seam in the limbs with ladder stitch. Once the head has been attached stuff the body, but not as firmly as the head, then close the gap in the seam with ladder stitch in the same way as for the limbs.

4 *Making the ears* Place the ears together in pairs with right sides facing and raw edges matching and backstitch all round the curved edge, leaving the straight edge open and your thread still attached. Turn each ear right sides out and ladder stitch across the opening, still leaving your thread attached. To attach each ear first insert your needle at the side of the head gusset where the top of the ear is to be. Ladder stitch the ear in position, turning the ear to point downwards after a few stitches. Stitch the front of the ear in place and then continue round the back of the ear.

5 *Attaching the limbs* Position the limbs and thread-joint them in the same way as for William, steps 3-4 (see page 25). Complete the bear by adding the nose and mouth and then gently brushing up the fur following steps 15-17 for Goldie on pages 17-18.

Making Alfred's waistcoat

1 *Stitching the waistcoat* Trace the pattern for Alfred's waistcoat from the pattern given left and use it to make a template. Cut the pattern from navy blue ultra suede, making sure you place it on a fabric fold as indicated. Fold the waistcoat in two places with right sides facing to match adjacent shoulder seams and stitch these two seams. Turn the waistcoat right sides out.

2 *Trimming the waistcoat* Cut two ⅛ x ⅜in (3 x 10mm) strips of red ultra suede and use slipstitch or oversewing to attach them to each front of the waistcoat. Alternatively, simply glue them in place. Fit the waistcoat on the bear and stitch the buttons on, securing the waistcoat front at the same time. If you wish, use a piece of brown Fimo or modelling clay to make a pipe for the bear to hold.

AMELIA

'It's astonishing, really, how many thoroughly mature, well-adjusted grown-ups harbour a teddy bear – which is perhaps why they are thoroughly mature and well-adjusted.'

JOSEPH LEMPA

Amelia is a bear who is constantly on the go and loves all kinds of sports and exercises, including cheerleading (see page 56). To help her get the best out of her activities she has special joints made from galvanised wire and washer replacements which enable her to take up more complicated poses than with traditional joints. This method of jointing, which was designed by Roberta Kasnick Ripperger of Creative Design Studio (see page 95), can be used with any bear pattern provided that its limbs are between 1in (2.5cm) and 2in (5cm) long. The washer replacements and wire must be used in conjunction with cotter pin joints and not thread joints.

FINISHED SIZE
3³/₄IN (9.5CM)

You will need

- 6 x 9in (15 x 23cm) piece of miniature bear fabric (American upholstery fabric, short-pile mohair or soft upholstery fabric)
- Matching ultra suede for paws and pads
- General-purpose sewing thread to match the bear fabric
- Black extra-strong nylon thread for attaching eyes
- Black stranded embroidery thread for the nose
- Black ultra suede for the nose
- Darning and fine sharp needles
- Polyester filling
- Pair of tiny (2mm) black beads for eyes
- Small round-nose pliers
- Long-nose tweezers
- Four ¼in (6mm) 'T' pin fibreboard cotter pin joints
- One ¼in (6mm) round pin fibreboard cotter pin joint
- Four washer replacements and galvanised wire (available from the Great British Bear Company)
- Stiletto
- Small teasel brush

Making Amelia

Trace the pattern pieces for Amelia from page 39 and use them to make card templates (see page 9). Transfer the paws and pads onto a single layer of ultra suede and cut out, adding an ⅛in (3mm) seam allowance around each piece. Transfer the remaining pieces onto the wrong side of a single layer of miniature bear fabric with the arrow on the pattern pointing in the direction of the fabric pile. Make sure you transfer the joint position marks onto the two body pieces and the appropriate arms and legs – this is most important. Cut out the pieces, adding an ⅛in (3mm) seam allowance around each one. Make the bear following the instructions below, using backstitch for seams and ladder stitch for closing seams (see page 10).

TIP – Teddy Tacks

Pins can often get in the way of the stitching when working with tiny bear pieces. So instead of using pins sew one or two large stitches to hold the fabric in place – teddy tacks. Then just pull them out when you have finished. It can be particularly helpful to work a teddy tack to secure the end of a seam – your stitching will secure the start.

1 *Starting the bear* With right sides facing backstitch the body pieces together and make the arms in the same way as for Goldie, steps 1-2 (page 13). Amelia only has two leg pieces instead of four. Fold each leg in half lengthways with right sides together and sew round the top of the leg from A to B. Work two or three extra stitches to take you round the corner and to avoid a square top of the leg. Then sew the top of the foot from C to D, leaving your needle and thread attached. Attach the foot pad following the instructions for Goldie, step 4. (page 14). Next make the head, add the eyes and ears and attach the head following steps 5–12 for Goldie (pages 14–17).

2 *Preparing the limb joints* Measure the length of each limb from the joint mark to the end of the limb. Double this figure and add ¼in (5mm) – for Amelia this makes 3in (7.5cm) for the legs and 2½in (6.5cm) for the arms. Cut the calculated length of wire for each limb. Using small round-nose pliers fold over ¼in (5mm) on each end of the wire (see below). Crimp the tops of the

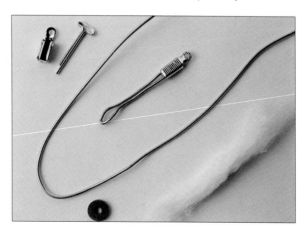

wire with the end folded back onto the wire then fold the wire in half, leaving a small gap so that a small amount of polyester filling can be inserted later.

 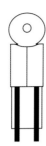

 Shaping the wire Insert the two crimped ends of wire into the bottom end of the washer replacement but do not allow them to cover up the hole at the top. Using the pliers again, squeeze down one of the sides of the washer replacement to stop the wire ends moving. Then roll the second side over the first flap and squeeze it shut, as shown, to make the whole assembly as narrow as possible. Put a small amount of polyester filling in the gap you left to cushion the end of the wire.

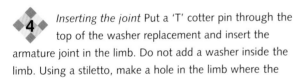

4 *Inserting the joint* Put a 'T' cotter pin through the top of the washer replacement and insert the armature joint in the limb. Do not add a washer inside the limb. Using a stiletto, make a hole in the limb where the

joint position is marked and insert the cotter pin. Now use the stiletto to make a hole in the body where the limb position is marked. Insert the cotter pin, protruding from the limb, then peel the fabric back so the cotter pin is accessible and put on the washer. Using a small cotter key or round-nose pliers open out the two ends of the cotter pin and bend each one round, back onto the washer. Check the limb is not too loose – if it is, use the small cotter key or round-nose pliers to bend the cotter pin ends round more. Fill the limb using long-nose tweezers to put the stuffing around the wire. Do not over-stuff and don't fill the body until all the jointing has been completed.

5 *Completing the bear* Fill the body, but not as firmly as the head, then work the nose and mouth following steps 15-16 for Goldie (pages 17-18) but using the photographs on page 36 as a guide. Brush the bear with a teasel brush to finish.

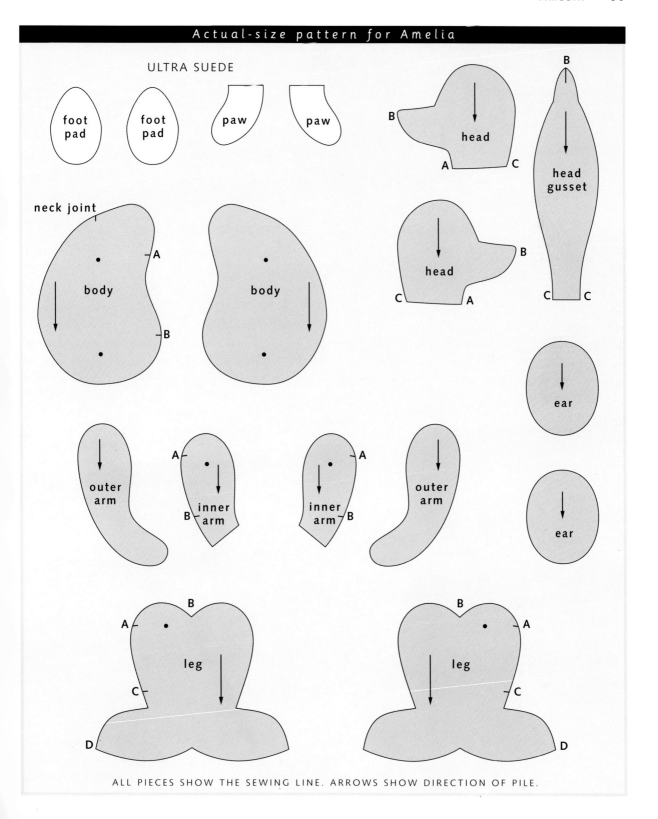

Actual-size pattern for Amelia

ULTRA SUEDE

ALL PIECES SHOW THE SEWING LINE. ARROWS SHOW DIRECTION OF PILE.

EDMUND

*'There is a personal relationship with teddy bears that never releases its grip.
Who can forget a real friend, perhaps the only friend who really understood?'*

BARBARA WERKMASTER, EVA-LENA BENGSSTON AND PER PETERSON

Edmund, like Amelia, is a sporty bear with the same armature so he can participate in many sports including golf (see page 59). His small, rounded nose gives him a very open, friendly expression and his soft fur makes him extremely cuddly. Make him from any short-pile miniature bear fabric or choose mohair fabric to give him a wind-swept look. However, if you do use mohair fabric don't forget to Fray Check (see page 51).

1 *Starting the bear* Join the body pieces and then make the arms, legs and head, adding the eyes and ears as you do so as for Goldie, steps 1-12 (pages 13-17). The limbs are attached with armature in the same way as Amelia's. Prepare the limb joints, shape the wire and attach the limbs following steps 2-4 for Amelia, pages 37-38.

FINISHED SIZE
3¾IN (9CM)

Making Edmund

You will need the same materials as for Amelia, see page 36. Trace the pattern pieces for Edmund given below and use them to make card templates (see page 9). Transfer the paws and pads onto a single layer of ultra suede and cut out, adding an $^1/_8$in (3mm) seam allowance around each piece. Transfer the remaining pieces onto the wrong side of a single layer of miniature bear fabric with the arrow on the pattern pointing in the direction of the fabric pile. Make sure you transfer the joint position marks onto the two body pieces and the appropriate arms and legs – this is most important. Cut out the pieces, adding an $^1/_8$in (3mm) seam allowance around each one. Make the bear following the instructions below using backstitch for seams and ladder stitch for closing seams (see page 10).

2 *Completing the bear* Fill the body, but not as firmly as the head, then work the nose following step 15 on page 17. To work an alternative mouth, bring the needle out at 1 (see right) and take a small stitch, going in at 4 and out at 1 again. Then go in at 5 and come out at 1. Pass the needle through to the back of the head and finish in the same way as in step 16, page 18.

TIP – Joint options

You may not need to use the joints given here in every limb – depending on how you wish to pose the bear you may be able to use ordinary joints in, say, the legs.

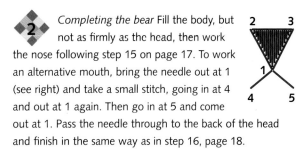

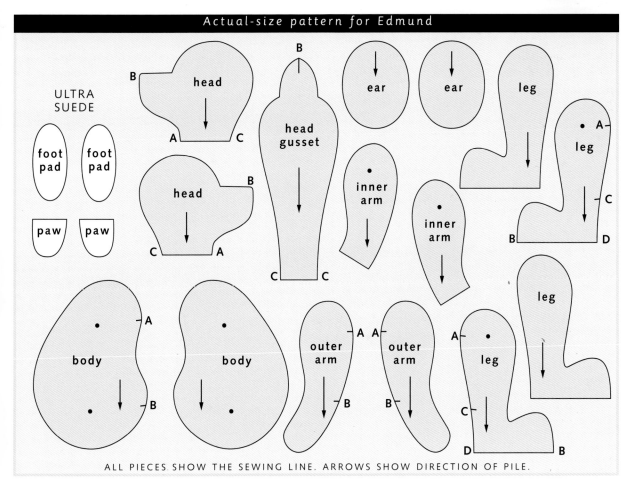

Actual-size pattern for Edmund

ULTRA SUEDE

foot pad   foot pad

paw   paw

head

head

head gusset

ear   ear   leg

leg

inner arm

inner arm

leg

body   body   outer arm   outer arm   leg

leg

ALL PIECES SHOW THE SEWING LINE. ARROWS SHOW DIRECTION OF PILE.

HUGO

'Even though there is a rip in your teddy bear, his love will not fall out.'

EVE FRANCES GIGLIOTTI

Hugo is an old bear with a suitably old-fashioned coat which you can make look more worn by following the tips at the end of this chapter. Alternatively you can make him from distressed mohair to start with which is available from some suppliers (see page 95).

This is a bear who looks as if he has been left alone in the attic for many years. He has a large tummy which you can make from contrasting bear fabric and a separate nose which you can also pick out in a contrasting fabric if you like. For a complete new look make his inner ears from the same contrasting fabric. Hugo is the largest bear in the book, standing a mighty 5in (13cm) tall and he is altogether a rather sturdy looking bear, which is just as well for him if he has been neglected for so long.

FINISHED SIZE
5IN (13CM)

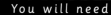
You will need

- 8in (20cm) square of light beige 100% mohair with a ¼in (7mm) pile
- Small piece of darker beige 100% mohair with a ¼in (7mm) pile for the tummy
- Ultra suede for paws and pads
- General-purpose sewing thread to match the main bear fabric
- Black extra-strong nylon thread for attaching eyes
- Black stranded embroidery thread for the nose
- Black ultra suede for the nose
- Darning and fine sharp needles
- Polyester filling
- Steel shot (optional)
- Pair of ¼in (5mm) glass bear eyes
- Five ⅝in (15mm) fibreboard cotter pin joints
- Round-nosed pliers
- Stiletto
- Small teasel brush
- Ribbon for trimming

Making Hugo

Trace the pattern pieces for Hugo from pages 44-45 and use them to make card templates (see page 9). Transfer the paws and pads onto a single layer of ultra suede and cut out, adding an $\frac{1}{8}$in (3mm) seam allowance around each piece. Transfer the tummy and, if you wish, the nose onto the wrong side of a single layer of the darker beige mohair and the remaining pieces onto the lighter mohair with the arrow on the pattern pointing in the direction of the fabric pile. There are no joint marks to transfer with this pattern. Cut out the pieces, adding an $\frac{1}{8}$in (3mm) seam allowance around each one. Make the bear following the instructions below, using backstitch for seams and ladder stitch for closing seams (see page 10).

1 *Preparing the body pieces* Take one body and the corresponding tummy piece and stitch together from A to B around the less curved edge of the tummy piece. You may find it easiest if you take a small stitch at each end before you begin. Repeat with the other body and tummy pieces. Now fold one body piece in half with right sides together so that the two edges of the dart at the top of the body match. Starting at the edge of the fabric backstitch along the dart, securing the thread well at the end. Turn the fabric over and check that the dart has created a pointed shape. Stitch the bottom dart in the same way and then stitch the two darts on the other body piece.

2 *Joining the body pieces* Now place the two body pieces together with right sides facing and raw edges matching and stitch from C to D. Finish the thread and rejoin it at E to stitch right round the bottom and tummy to F. Using extra-strong nylon thread, work running stitch around the top of the body, pull up tight and secure the thread. Turn the body right sides out through the gap in the back.

 3 *Making the limbs and head* Make the arms and legs following steps 2-4 for Goldie on pages 13-14. To assemble the head take the head gusset and one head piece and with right sides facing and raw edges matching stitch the seam from A round the curved edge of the head to B. Sew the remaining head piece to the other side of the head gusset in the same way. Now fold the nose in half and line up the centre mark on the nose with the centre mark on the head gusset. With right sides together stitch from the centre of the nose to C. Return to the centre and stitch to D. Then sew from the tip of the nose to E at the edge of the head. Turn the head right sides out and stuff firmly, starting with the nose.

 4 *Adding the eyes* Sculpt the eye sockets following step 8 for Goldie (page 14). Larger eyes, like these, usually have looped backs. To attach them it is necessary to pinch the round loops together with round-nose pliers to enable them to fit into the hole in the fabric. Start by pinching the loop where it actually goes into the glass eye, working out towards the end of the wire loop. Be very

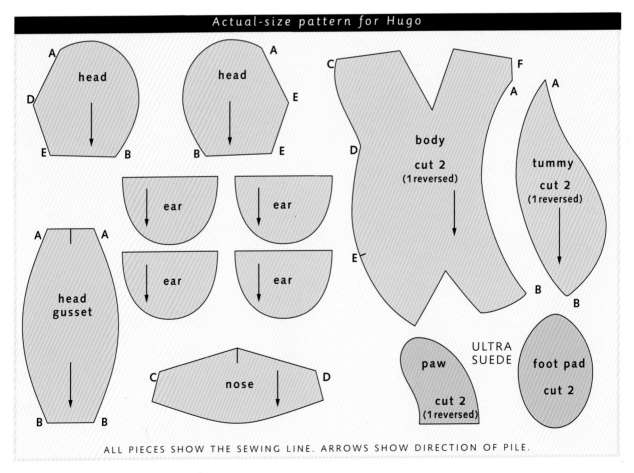

Actual-size pattern for Hugo

ALL PIECES SHOW THE SEWING LINE. ARROWS SHOW DIRECTION OF PILE.

gentle or the eye will shatter. Then make a hole where each eye is to be inserted using a stiletto. Thread a long needle with a double length of extra-strong nylon thread and insert it into the head from the base, bringing it out through one hole. Thread on an eye and take the needle back through the hole and out at the base of the head. Pull firmly and knot the ends together. Attach the other eye in the same way. Tie just one knot with the two sets of threads and then pull the threads very tightly so the eyes embed themselves in their sockets. Keep a firm tension on the threads and tie off securely with several knots. Cut off the threads and then bury the ends inside the head. You can also use the method on page 16 to insert looped-back eyes.

5 *Attaching the ears* Prepare the head joint and attach the head to the body following steps 10-11 for Goldie (page 16). To assemble the ears simply place two ear pieces together with right sides facing and raw edges matching and stitch around the curved edge, leaving the straight edge open. Turn right sides out and ladder stitch across the open edge before attaching the ears (see step 12 for Goldie, page 17).

6 *Completing the bear* Finish the bear following the instructions for Goldie, steps 13-17 (pages 17-18). I used steel shot as a filling to give that 'saggy bear' look. This also gives the bear added weight and makes it quite poseable. However, it is unlikely that the

TIP - Using steel shot

Ensure that the shot is the type that will not rust. Use a small glass phial (test tube) or teaspoon to help you fill the bear and do not over-fill, particularly if you want to obtain a 'saggy bear' look.

Actual-size pattern for Hugo

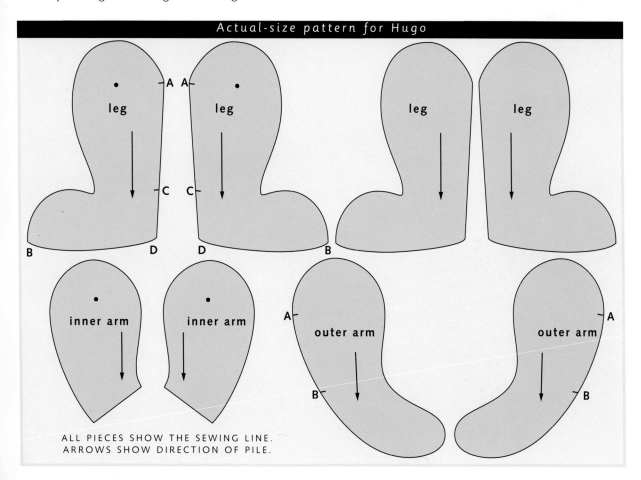

leg leg leg leg

inner arm inner arm outer arm outer arm

ALL PIECES SHOW THE SEWING LINE.
ARROWS SHOW DIRECTION OF PILE.

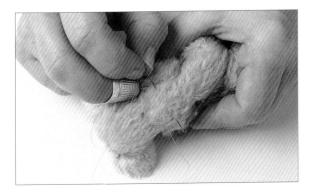

bear will stand up easily if you fill it with steel shot, so consider how you want your bear to pose before stuffing it. If your bear has a hump insert a little polyester filling into this area first with long tweezers. Using matching thread and starting inside the tummy cavity with a knot, bring the needle out at the side of the hump, take a tiny stitch and pass the needle to the other side of the hump. Do not pull tightly or you will create a dimple. Repeat two or three times to hold the filling in place. Then fill the body cavity with steel shot before closing the back seam. You must work the ladder stitch close together to avoid the steel shot escaping. You can use steel shot in the limbs too, although this isn't so important, but if so insert a little polyester filling into the pads and paws first and stitch in place before adding the steel shot.

7 *Adding claws* You can give claws to Hugo or indeed any of the bears in this book. Use one strand of black embroidery thread with a small knot. Insert the needle into the arm and 'pop' the knot inside. Bring the needle out at A on the paw pad. Insert it at B and bring it out at C, then insert it at D and bring it out at E. Finally, insert the needle at F and bring it out further up the arm to finish the thread with a knot which can then be lost in the arm. Repeat on the other paw and both foot pads. You can trim the bear with a bow, but remember that he is supposed to be old, so you don't want it looking too pristine.

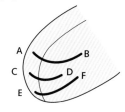

Making a bear look distressed

Here are some ideas for 'aging' your finished bear:

✤ Sew a patch on your bear using a bear fabric in a slightly different colour and just before you finish attaching it put some stuffing under the patch and leave a little poking out.

✤ Tie a piece of frayed fabric round an arm or leg to look like the remains of a garment. Sew on the fabric with invisible stitches but allow it to look tied on. You could even add a tiny safety pin to look as though it is holding the fabric in place.

✤ Roll up a scrap of polyester filling and stitch it to the bear so that it looks as if it is sticking out. Try stitching it over a seam or make it look as if there is a hole in the bear. (Obviously you shouldn't actually cut a hole in your bear – just aim to give that impression.)

ACTION BEARS

Incorporating armature into the construction of your bears makes it possible to display them in a wide variety of poses. This gives potential for a whole new range of action bears and in particular those involved in sporting activities. Find out how to make a ballerina, American footballer, cheerleader, golfer, cricketer, skier, fishing bear and tennis player, or adapt any of these sporting bears to suit your own favourite pastimes, taking team colours and so on into account.

BASES

When positioning the bears it may be necessary to anchor them on a base. You can make any shape of fabric base by following or adapting the method given here. Wait until you have completed the bear before you make the base and ideally insert pins for it to stand on before attaching the lining (see step 2).

Making an oval or round base

1 *Covering the base* Cut an oval or round piece of mount board which is the finished size required. A cake base available from most cake decorating suppliers is ideal. These come in many shapes and size and are usually quite reasonably priced. Cut a piece of fabric 1in (2.5cm) larger than the board all the way round. Work running stitch around the edge of the fabric and then gently pull up the thread. Insert the piece of board and pull up the gathering thread to fit neatly and smoothly over the top. Secure the gathering thread.

2 *Securing the bears* If you can ascertain where the bears will stand on the base it is a good idea to insert two short pins approximately ½in (1.25cm) apart for each bear before stitching the lining to the bottom of the base. Use an awl to make the holes and then insert the pins from the underside, coming up through the top of the base. Your bears will stand on the pins.

3 *Lining the base* Cut a piece of fine cardboard which is ¼in (6mm) smaller all the way round than the finished base. Cut another piece of fabric 1in (2.5cm) larger all round than the cardboard and cover it in the same way as in step 1 but do not secure the gathering thread. Instead, press the fabric and then remove the cardboard. Place the gathered fabric on the underside of the main base with the wrong side facing the board. Ladder stitch the two pieces together, leaving the board in the middle. This covers all the raw edges and makes a very neat covered base.

Making a square or oblong base

Make a square or oblong base in the same way as an oval or round one but mitre the fabric at the corners rather than gathering it up with running stitch. You should be able to shape the lining without using a cardboard template.

Making a small round wooden base

If you have a bear who is reluctant to stand, a small base may be the answer. Cut a 1½in (4cm) diameter circle from ⅛in 3mm thick plywood. Using an awl or fine drill make two holes approximately ½in (1.25cm) apart. Stain or varnish the wooden base and then insert two short pins from the underside ready to stand your bear on. Cut and attach a piece of Fablon (self-adhesive baize) to fit the underside or glue on a piece of felt. This neatens the underside and stops the base from wobbling because of the pin heads. It also protects your tabletop from being scratched by the pins. When it is completely dry, stand your bear on the pins which will go up his legs.

DANCING ON POINTS

'A bear, however hard he tries, grows tubby without exercise.'

FROM 'TEDDY BEAR' BY A. A. MILNE

Balancing confidently on both points and with arms in a graceful sweep in front of her, this beautiful bear has just finished a series of arabesques and is about to meet with thunderous applause. Standing approximately 4in (10cm) tall on her points, the bear is beautifully clothed in beaded tutu with a necklace, feathered tiara and pretty pink ballet shoes – she's every little girl's dream. Her fur is made from soft honey-brown miniature bear upholstery fabric to give her a very feminine look, while her paws are made from pale ultra suede.

To help her hold her position the bear's arms are positioned slightly lower than normal, ⅙in (3mm) lower than the joint marks given on the pattern (see page 39). Her feet are obviously also different but they are easy to stitch because there are no pads.

You will need

- ✣ 6 x 9in (15 x 23cm) piece of miniature bear fabric (American upholstery fabric, short-pile mohair or soft upholstery fabric)
- ✣ Matching ultra suede for paws
- ✣ Scrap of pink ultra suede for the ballet shoes
- ✣ General-purpose sewing thread to match the main fabric
- ✣ Extra-strong black nylon thread
- ✣ Black stranded embroidery thread for the nose
- ✣ Black ultra suede for the nose
- ✣ Darning and fine sharp needles
- ✣ Polyester filling
- ✣ Pair of ⅛in (3mm) matching black beads or bear eyes
- ✣ Four ¼in (6mm) 'T' pin fibreboard cotter pin joints
- ✣ One ¼in (6mm) round pin fibreboard cotter pin joint
- ✣ Two washer replacements (four if you wish to add armature to the legs too)
- ✣ Galvanised wire
- ✣ Small teasel brush

For trimming the ballerina

- ✣ 4 x 6in (10 x 15cm) piece of fine white tulle
- ✣ 1 x 5in (2.5 x 13cm) piece of fine white chiffon
- ✣ 3½in (9cm) length of lace 1in (2.5cm) wide for her underwear
- ✣ Extra-strong white nylon thread
- ✣ Nylon monofil sewing thread (invisible thread)
- ✣ Light pink stranded embroidery thread to match the pink ultra suede
- ✣ Small white pearl beads
- ✣ Small gold beads
- ✣ Small translucent pink beads for trimming the tutu
- ✣ Small white feather for the tiara
- ✣ Tiny white flowers (optional) such as those used for cake decorating
- ✣ Narrow white picot braid
- ✣ 2½in (6cm) of ¾in (2cm) wide white satin ribbon

Making the ballerina

Trace the pattern pieces for Amelia from page 39, omitting the legs and foot pads, then trace the additional pieces for the ballerina given right and use them to make card templates (see page 9). Transfer the paws and feet onto a single layer of ultra suede and cut out, adding an ⅛in (3mm) seam allowance around each piece. Using the legs given here, transfer the remaining pieces onto the wrong side of a single layer of miniature bear fabric. Make sure you transfer the joint position marks onto the two body pieces and the arms and legs; the arms must be ⅛in (3mm) lower than marked. Cut out the pieces, adding an ⅛in (3mm) seam allowance around each one. Make the bear following the instructions below, using backstitch for seams and ladder stitch for closing seams (see page 10).

Actual-size pattern for the ballerina

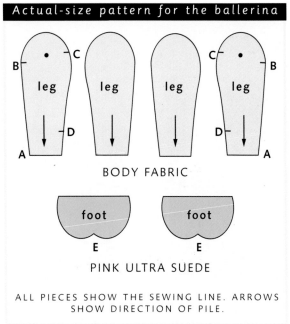

BODY FABRIC

PINK ULTRA SUEDE

ALL PIECES SHOW THE SEWING LINE. ARROWS SHOW DIRECTION OF PILE.

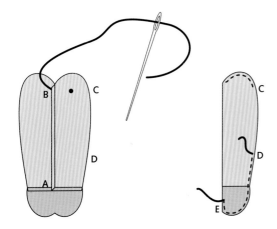

1 *Getting started* With right sides facing and raw edges matching backstitch the body pieces together and make the arms in the same way as for Goldie, steps 1-2 (page 13). Pin the legs together in pairs with right sides facing and backstitch from A to B at the thigh but leave the thread attached. Open out and, with right sides facing, use a new length of thread to sew one pink ultra suede foot to the bottom of each leg piece with the seam you have just sewn positioned in the centre of the ultra suede. Press the seam open. Fold the leg in half with right sides facing and raw edges matching and use the attached thread to continue sewing from B to C. Finish the thread off and then stitch from D to E on the foot, continuing around the curve for a few stitches at E, as shown, to produce a smooth curve. Turn right sides out.

2 *Completing the bear* Make and attach the head and add the eyes and ears following steps 5-12 for Goldie (pages 14-17). Insert armature in the arms following steps 2-4 for Amelia (pages 37-38) and add the legs following step 13 for Goldie (page 17) or using armature in the same way as you did for the arms. Finish the bear following steps 14-17 for Goldie (pages 17-18).

TIP – Strengthening your thread

Run your thread over a block of beeswax before sewing with it. This strengthens the thread and also prevents it becoming knotted.

Dressing the ballerina

1 *Making the tutu* To make the top of the tutu fold the white satin ribbon in half and neatly oversew down both sides. Sew a piece of narrow white picot braid along the fold and decorate with translucent pink beads. Work four French knots (see page 10) down the centre of the ribbon using one strand of light pink embroidery thread. Then attach a 3in (8cm) length of white picot braid to both sides of the top for the shoulder straps. (It will help if you check the positioning of the straps by fitting the top on the bear first). Place the top of the tutu on the bear and stitch in position along the bottom of the satin ribbon. Cross the straps over on the back of the bear and stitch in place. The ends of the straps will be hidden by the ballet skirt.

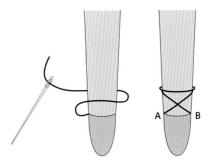

2 *Finishing the shoes* To turn the bear's feet into shoes take a long needle and thread it with three strands of light pink embroidery thread; tie a knot in the end. Put your needle in at the top back of the bear's leg and bring it out at the side of the foot, just where the pink ultra suede joins the bear fabric at A. Wrap the thread round the leg once and then cross it over at the front and insert the needle back into the leg on the other side of the ballet shoe at B, bringing it out again at the top of the leg, preferably at the back. Tie a knot and run it down to the fabric. Do not pull the knots back into the leg because it may pull the thread too tight on the front; the knots will be hidden by the undies. Repeat to thread laces on the other foot.

TIP – Fray prevention

If I am using a fabric that frays badly (for either the bear or the costume) I treat it very lightly with Fray Check crystals before I begin work. You can do the same with your fabric. It is important to use only a light sprinkling of Fray Check crystals or the fabric will go very stiff which makes it difficult to sew. See Suppliers, page 95 for where to obtain Fray Check crystals.

3 *Making the underwear* To make the undies place the 3½in (9cm) length of lace round the bear's waist and join at the back of the bear with a small seam. Stitch the lace together between the bear's legs. To make the underskirt use white extra-strong nylon thread to work a small running stitch along the edge of the white chiffon and pull up the stitches to gather it. Now place the chiffon round the bear's middle, over the top of the tutu and ribbon ends, so that the ends of the chiffon meet at the back of the bear. There is no need to stitch the ends together. Secure the gathering thread tightly.

4 *Finishing the tutu* Fold the tulle in half lengthways (2 x 6in) and then in half again (1 x 6in). Trim along the folds. Use white nylon thread to work a small running stitch along the centre. Pull up the thread to gather the tulle and place the skirt on the bear, over the chiffon, so that the ends meet at the back. (It is not necessary to sew the join because the ends will be secured when beads are added later.) Fasten the gathering thread tightly and smooth down the skirt. Using nylon monofil invisible thread attach translucent pink beads randomly on

the tutu. Do not pull the thread too tightly because it will gather up the fabric. When you reach the end of the tulle catch the two ends together and add a bead then knot securely. Go into the top of the bear's leg, come out on the other side and cut off the thread end.

5 *Adding the jewellery and tiara* Thread some small pearl beads onto a length of extra-strong white nylon thread to make a necklace and place it round the bear's neck; secure the ends. Sew one pearl bead to each ear for earrings, using the photograph as a guide to positioning. To make the feathered tiara thread 10 beads onto a length of extra-strong white nylon thread, alternating white pearls and gold beads. Attach it to the bear's head between the ears. Add a few tiny white flowers or beads and finally a small white feather to complete the tiara. Bend the arms towards the front of the bear and use matching thread to sew the two paws together to hold the dancer's position.

TOUCH DOWN

'Cuddly and warm, these calming creatures reassure me in the days of doubt when fears fly before reason and the world looms bleak instead of beautiful.'

ANONYMOUS

With its larger-than-life personalities and its equally large physiques and salaries, American football is rapidly gaining a following all over the world. Many of us can't claim to understand the game, but we are all touched by its glamour and a sporting selection of bears wouldn't be complete without a player. Don't worry, though, if you aren't interested in the American game you can easily adapt the player as a British footballer – simply assemble the bear's legs in bear-coloured

fabric then make the shorts and T-shirt in team colours and omit the body armour.

Our player is made from light beige 100% mohair with matching ultra suede paws. His legs are made from red ultra suede to give the look of clothing and his feet are made from white ultra suede which is painted to give a shiny finish. He sports the necessary protection in the form of shoulder and knee pads and helmet. You may also like to stitch his cheerleader (see page 56).

You will need

+ 6 x 9in (15 x 23cm) piece of light beige 100% mohair fabric
+ Matching ultra suede for paws
+ Small piece of red ultra suede for the legs
+ White ultra suede for the shoes
+ Black ultra suede for the nose
+ General-purpose sewing thread to match main fabric
+ Extra-strong black nylon thread
+ Black stranded embroidery thread for the nose
+ Darning and fine sharp needles
+ Polyester filling
+ Pair of ⅛in (3mm) matching black beads or bear eyes
+ Four ¼in (6mm) 'T' pin fibreboard cotter pin joints
+ One ¼in (6mm) round pin fibreboard cotter pin joint
+ Four washer replacements
+ Galvanised wire
+ Small teasel brush

For dressing the American footballer
+ Soft red fabric for the shirt (an old football shirt is ideal)
+ Navy blue stretch fabric for the shorts
+ Narrow ribbon to trim the shorts
+ White felt for pads
+ White extra-strong thread plus red/black thread
+ Embroidery cotton to work the shirt's number
+ Table-tennis ball for the helmet
+ Black 2.5mm thick wire
+ Black insulation tape
+ Acrylic varnish such as Mod Podge
+ Sharp craft knife
+ Cling film
+ Fabric stiffener or a solution of 50:50 PVA glue to water
+ Instant-bonding adhesive

Making the American footballer

Trace the pattern pieces for Edmund from page 41, omitting the legs and foot pads, then trace the additional body pieces for the footballer from page 55 and use them to make card templates (see page 9). Transfer the paws, legs and feet onto a single layer of ultra suede and cut out, adding an ⅛in (3mm) seam allowance around each piece. Transfer the remaining pieces onto the wrong side of a single layer of miniature bear fabric. Make sure you transfer the joint position marks onto the two body pieces and the appropriate arms and legs – this is most important. Cut out the pieces, adding an ⅛in (3mm) seam allowance around each one. Make the bear following the instructions below, using backstitch for seams and ladder stitch for closing seams (see page 10).

1 *Getting started* With right sides facing and raw edges matching stitch the body pieces together and make the arms in the same way as for Goldie, steps 1-2 (page 13). The legs are longer than normal and do not have foot pads. First use red thread to attach the straight part of the top edge of a white foot to the straight lower edge of each red leg, stitching from A to B. You should have two feet facing one way and two facing the other way. Now place the legs together in pairs with right sides facing and raw edges matching. Stitch from C round the top of the leg to D using red thread. Finish off the thread. Now stitch from E to F, change to white thread and stitch from F to C. Turn the legs out through the gap.

TIP – Quick patterns

You can save time by tracing the pattern pieces directly onto template film instead of using tracing paper and card. Template film is a stiff, clear plastic available from patchwork shops. Use a fine permanent marker to trace the pattern and label it carefully. Template film is designed for tracing hundreds of pieces of fabric for patchwork so it lasts well. Cut it with scissors and switch to a craft knife and metal ruler to cut straight edges.

2 *Completing the bear* Make and attach the head and add the eyes and ears following steps 5-12 for Goldie (pages 14-17). Insert armature in the arms and legs following steps 2-4 for Amelia (pages 37-38), then finish the bear following steps 14-17 for Goldie (pages 17-18).

Dressing the American footballer

1 *Cutting out the pieces* Trace the patterns for the T-shirt, shorts, shoulder pads and shin pads from page 55 and use them to make card templates. (There is no need to make a pattern of the helmet.) Cut the shoulder pads and shin pads from white felt (seam allowances are not required). Now cut the shirt from red stretch fabric and the shorts from navy stretch fabric or use your team colours – again the pattern line is the cutting line.

2 *Making the shin pads* You need to stiffen and shape the shin pads before stitching them to the bear. To make a mould, cover a pen that is approximately

FINISHED SIZE
3½IN (9CM)

½in (12mm) in diameter with cling film. Soak the shin pads in fabric stiffener or glue solution and squeeze out the excess then smooth them over the pen. Put a second piece of cling film over the top and smooth it down. After ten minutes carefully remove the top layer of cling film and leave the pads to dry for 2-3 hours in a warm place. When they are dry carefully ease the felt off and trim slightly if necessary. Use white extra-strong thread to stitch the pads to the bear, making two holes midway up the pad. Go back and forth twice using the same holes and taking the thread round the back of the bear's legs.

3 *Making the shoulder pads* Soak the shoulder pads in glue solution or fabric stiffener and shape the shoulders in the same way as the shin pads – you don't need the cling film because this piece is much bigger. When the felt is dry make a cut down the centre front to the neck opening and place the pads on the bear. Check the fit and trim the pads slightly, if necessary. Join the front edges of the shoulder pads with ladder stitch using white thread and taking your stitches into the bear to make sure that the pads are secure.

4 *Making the T-shirt* Cut the back of the shirt down the middle as far as the neck opening. Make a small snip into the fabric at the front V of the neck opening and at the shoulder points, then fold back the four edges of the neck; stitch in place to neaten the neck. Turn a tiny hem on the sleeve edges BB and DD and stitch in place too. Fold the shirt at the shoulders and stitch the underarm side seams AB and CD. If your fabric frays, hem the shirt. Use minute chain stitch to embroider a number on the front of the shirt and/or on the sleeve. Fit the shirt on the bear and close the back seam with ladder stitch.

5 *Making the shorts* Stitch a tiny hem along the bottom edge of each shorts leg. Place the two pieces together with right sides facing and raw edges matching and stitch from A to B and then from C to D. Sew from DB to E along each leg. Turn the shorts out and fit on the bear with A at the front waist and C at the back waist. Stitch the inside leg seams to complete the legs. Tuck under a tiny hem at the waist and stitch if desired, although it should stay put once the shirt is tucked in. A narrow ribbon stitched around the bottom of the shorts legs will give an extra-smart finish.

6 *Finishing the shoes* Use red or black thread to work three or four stitches across the white ultra suede feet to represent the shoe laces. As a final touch apply two or three coats of acrylic varnish to give the shoes a shiny finish, following the manufacturer's instructions.

7 *Making the helmet* Draw the helmet design given opposite onto a table-tennis ball and carefully cut it out with a sharp craft knife. To make the face guard bend a 3½in (9cm) length of black wire in half, leaving a small gap between the two halves. Curve the wire to run from one side of the helmet to the other then secure with instant-bonding adhesive. Stick a narrow strip of black insulating tape from the top of the head to the back of the neck on the helmet.

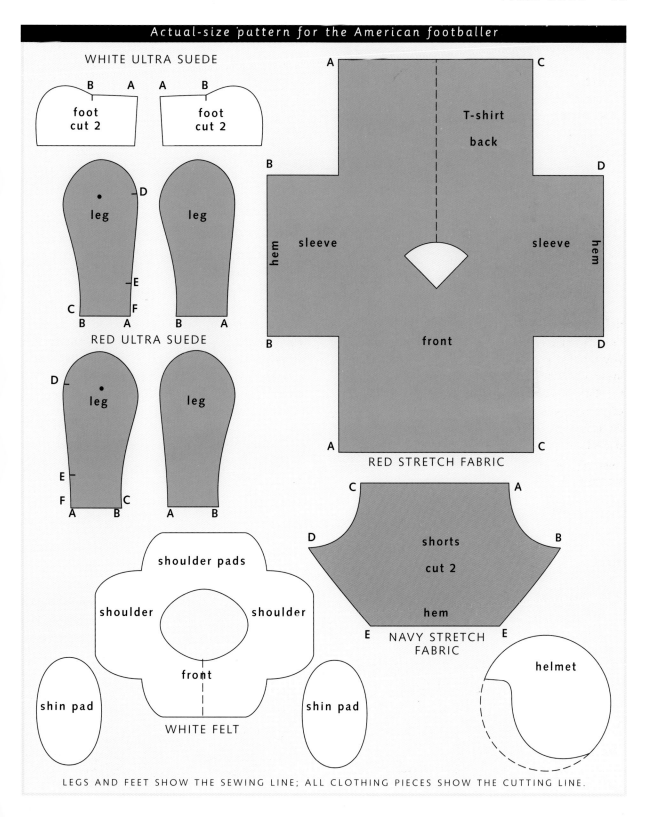

Actual-size pattern for the American footballer

WHITE ULTRA SUEDE

foot cut 2

foot cut 2

A   C

T-shirt

back

B   D

hem   sleeve   sleeve   hem

front

A   C

RED STRETCH FABRIC

leg

D

E

F

C   F
B   A

leg

B   A

RED ULTRA SUEDE

D

leg

E

F   C
A   B

leg

A   B

C   A

shorts

cut 2

D   B

hem

E   NAVY STRETCH   E
FABRIC

shoulder pads

shoulder   shoulder

front

WHITE FELT

shin pad

shin pad

helmet

LEGS AND FEET SHOW THE SEWING LINE; ALL CLOTHING PIECES SHOW THE CUTTING LINE.

TWO, FOUR, SIX, EIGHT

*'Teddy bears make great confessors, advisors, best friends – and scapegoats.
Whenever my mother prepared to punish me for one misdeed or another,
I would always be ready with "Teddy did it!"'*

ANONYMOUS

No American football match would be complete without its cheerleaders. They encourage the team players and entertain the crowds, often performing some spectacular gymnastics, so our girl is fully fitted out with armature to enable her to move with the best

of them. She wears a white cropped top, white undies and a blue and red skirt which twirls as she moves and she waves two bright pompons. Feathers in her hair and sparkling anklets complete the look.

The cheerleader is based on Amelia. The only difference is that she has contrasting pale paws and pads, but you can make the bear with matching paws if you prefer and then dress her in the cheerleader's costume. The bear is 3¾in (9.5cm) tall.

Making the cheerleader

Trace the pattern pieces for Amelia from page 39 and use them to make card templates (see page 9). Transfer the paws and pads onto a single layer of ultra suede and cut out, adding an ⅛in (3mm) seam allowance around each piece. Transfer the remaining pieces onto the wrong side of a single layer of miniature bear fabric with the arrow on the pattern pointing in the direction of the fabric pile. Make sure you transfer the joint position marks onto the two body pieces and the appropriate arms and legs – this is most important. Cut out the pieces, adding an ⅛in (3mm) seam allowance around each one. Make the bear following the instructions for Amelia on pages 37-38, using backstitch for seams and ladder stitch for closing seams (see page 10).

FINISHED SIZE
3¾IN (9.5CM)

- ❖ 6 x 9in (15 x 23cm) piece of miniature bear fabric (American upholstery fabric, short-pile mohair or soft upholstery fabric)
- ❖ Contrasting ultra suede for paws and pads
- ❖ General-purpose sewing thread to match bear fabric
- ❖ Black extra-strong nylon thread for attaching eyes
- ❖ Black stranded embroidery thread for the nose
- ❖ Black ultra suede for the nose
- ❖ Darning and fine sharp needles
- ❖ Polyester filling
- ❖ Pair of tiny (2mm) black beads for eyes
- ❖ Small round-nose pliers
- ❖ Long-nose tweezers
- ❖ Four ¼in (6mm) 'T' pin fibreboard cotter pin joints
- ❖ One ¼in (6mm) round pin fibreboard cotter pin joint
- ❖ Galvanised wire

- ❖ Four washer replacements (available from the Great British Bear Company)
- ❖ Stiletto
- ❖ Small teasel brush

For dressing the cheerleader
- ❖ Soft nylon fabric in red and blue
- ❖ White felt for the cropped top
- ❖ Lightweight interfacing for the cropped top
- ❖ Fine white knitted fabric for the undies
- ❖ Fine red and gold picot braid
- ❖ Blue thread to trim the top
- ❖ Red, white and blue tissue paper (or use felt-tip pens to colour strips of white tissue)
- ❖ Cocktail stick
- ❖ Clear glue such as Hi-Tack All Purpose Glue
- ❖ Red and blue feathers

Dressing the cheerleader

1 *Cutting out the pieces* Trace the patterns for the clothes given below, right and use them to make card templates. Use your templates to cut four skirt pieces from blue nylon fabric and four from red nylon fabric. Cut the waistband from red nylon fabric, placing it on a fold as indicated, and the undies from white stretch fabric. Now iron interfacing onto white felt and use this to cut the two pieces for the cheerleader's top.

2 *Making the skirt* Join alternate blue and red skirt panels together to make one long strip. Fold the waistband in half lengthways with wrong sides together. Lay out the joined skirt and place the waistband on top so that its long raw edges line up with the top raw edges of the skirt. Stitch this seam and stitch up the two short ends of the waistband. Fold the waistband up and press with your fingers. Stitch the open side seam from the bottom edge to about halfway up. Slip the skirt onto the bear then close the seam with ladder stitch. Seal the hem with a little glue, if desired.

3 *Making the undies* Apply a little glue to the top long edge of each piece, turn 2mm and seal to the wrong side. Seal the curved leg openings in the same way. When the glue has dried place the two pieces together with right sides facing and raw edges matching. Stitch the side seams from A to B and from C to D, then stitch the lower seam to finish. Turn the undies right sides out and slip them on the bear.

4 *Stitching the top* Couch the blue thread a little way up from the lower edge of each top piece, making sure the trim is level on both pieces. Place the two pieces together with right sides facing and stitch the shoulder and side seam on one side only. Turn the top right sides out and fit it on the bear then ladder stitch the open seams closed. Tie picot braid around the neck to finish.

BACK VIEW

5 *Trimming the bear* Make the anklets by stitching a small piece of red and gold picot braid round each ankle and finishing the ends neatly at the back. For her feathers first pull out tiny feather filaments in red and blue and form two balanced bunches. Secure each bunch by whipping the ends together tightly with sewing thread, then stitch the bunches on the bear's head (see photograph on page 56).

6 *Making the pompons* Cut three strips of tissue, one red, one blue and one white, each ¾ x 5in (2 x 12.5cm). Stack them and make ⅛in (2mm) parallel cuts ½in (12mm) deep into one long edge. Apply glue to one end of each strip (still stacked) and attach it close to one end of a cocktail stick, as shown – leave enough cocktail stick at the uncut end of the tissue to form a handle for the bear to hold. Roll the tissue very tightly along the stick, then glue the ends. Fold back the paper and cut off the cocktail stick in the centre of the pompon. Fluff up the tissue and attach the pompon's handle to the bear's paw. Repeat to make a second pompon in the same way.

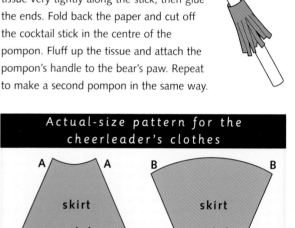

Actual-size pattern for the cheerleader's clothes

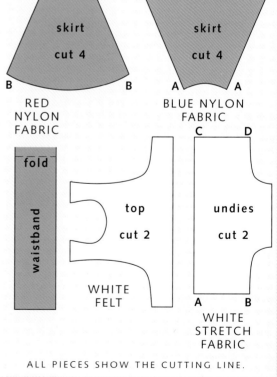

A   A   B   B

skirt
cut 4

skirt
cut 4

B   B   A   A

RED NYLON FABRIC   BLUE NYLON FABRIC

fold

waistband

WHITE FELT

top
cut 2

C   D

undies
cut 2

A   B

WHITE STRETCH FABRIC

ALL PIECES SHOW THE CUTTING LINE.

HOLE IN ONE

'Mr Teddy was there when I had no friends to play with, no one to talk to, no one to share my little woes or my big joys. ... Now when I see him on the shelf, he is like my flesh and my soul – older, worn, but still full of happiness.'

ROBERT KUNCIOV

On his weekends our bear likes nothing better than a good game of golf. His special joints enable him to get an excellent back swing and give him all the precision he needs for a fine putt. He wears traditional checked trousers and leather peaked cap with a sweater to keep out the chill without restricting arm movement. His golf shoes are made from two colours of leather, although you could use a single colour if you prefer. Name your golfer bear after your favourite player or call him Tiger after Tiger Woods in the hope that he will reach the peak of his sport at a very early age.

Making the golfer

Trace the pattern pieces for Edmund from page 41 and use them to make card templates (see page 9). Transfer the paws and pads onto a single layer of ultra suede and cut out, adding an ¹/₈in (3mm) seam allowance around each piece. Transfer the remaining pieces onto the wrong side of a single layer of miniature bear fabric with the arrow on the pattern pointing in the direction of the fabric pile. Make sure you transfer the joint position marks onto the two body pieces and the appropriate arms and legs – this is most important. Cut out the pieces, adding an ¹/₈in (3mm) seam allowance around each one. Make the bear following the instructions on pages 40-41 using backstitch for seams and ladder stitch for closing seams (see page 10).

FINISHED SIZE
3¹/₂IN (9CM)

- 6 x 9in (15 x 23cm) piece of miniature bear fabric (American upholstery fabric, short-pile mohair or soft upholstery fabric)
- Matching ultra suede for paws and pads
- General-purpose sewing thread to match the bear fabric
- Black extra-strong nylon thread for attaching the eyes
- Black stranded embroidery thread for the nose
- Black ultra suede for the nose
- Darning and fine sharp needles
- Polyester filling
- Pair of ⅛in (3mm) black beads for eyes
- Small round-nose pliers
- Long-nose tweezers
- Four ¼in (6mm) 'T' pin fibreboard cotter pin joints
- One ¼in (6mm) round pin fibreboard cotter pin joint
- Galvanised wire

- Four washer replacements (available from the Great British Bear Company)
- Stiletto
- Small teasel brush

For dressing the golfer
- Small-scale checked fabric for the trousers
- Cotton fabric for the cap lining – or use the trouser fabric
- Soft fabric for the sweater
- Scraps of leather in two colours for the shoes and cap
- Green felt for the collar
- Embroidery thread for the sweater (see step 4)
- Extra-long cooks' match or a wooden skewer for the golf club
- Brown and white Fimo or modelling clay
- Black insulating tape or woven tape
- Nylon monofil invisible thread

Dressing the golfer

1 *Cutting out the pieces* Trace the patterns for the trousers, cap, shoes, collar and sweater, given below, and use them to make card templates. Use your templates to cut two trousers from checked fabric and the collar from green felt. Fold a piece of soft fabric in half and use it to cut out the sweater, placing the template on the fabric fold as indicated. Cut one cap peak from leather and one from cotton fabric and the cap crown from folded leather. Cut the shoes from leather, too.

2 *Making the trousers* Turn and stitch a small hem along the bottom of each trouser leg from E to E. Pin the two trouser legs together with right sides facing and raw edges matching and stitch from A to B and from C to

D. Now fold the fabric so you can sew from DB to E along each leg. Turn the trousers right sides out and fit onto the bear. Turn under a small hem around the bear's waist and then take a few small stitches at the back of the trousers to take in the fullness. Work a few stitches at the front and back of the waist to attach the trousers to the bear.

3 *Making the sweater* Cut the sweater to the neck opening from C to D so you can fit it on the bear. Turn and stitch a small hem along the wrist edge of each sleeve BB and along the front and back edges AA and AC. Fold the sweater in half through the centre of each sleeve so the straight edge of the neck opening runs along the fold and stitch each side/sleeve seam from A to B. Turn the sweater right sides out and fit it on the bear with the open seam at the back. Stitch this seam closed with ladder stitch.

Actual-size pattern for the golfer's clothes

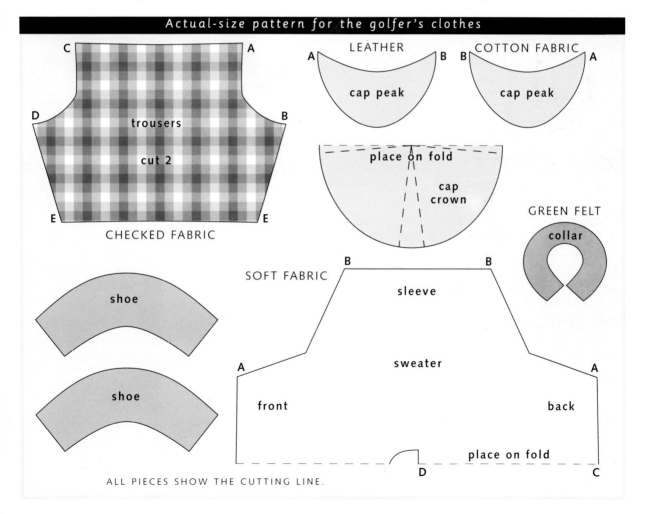

ALL PIECES SHOW THE CUTTING LINE.

◆**4** *Adding the collar* Place the collar around the bear's neck over the sweater and stitch the fronts together. Catch the collar down at the back of the bear's neck too. Using one strand of contrasting embroidery thread stitch a small shape on the top of one sleeve and on the same side of the sweater front. Add another colour to highlight the motif.

◆**5** *Making the cap* Place the two cap peaks together with right sides facing and raw edges matching and stitch around the curve from A to B. Turn right sides out and press. Fold the crown in half with right sides together and stitch the darts from the edge to the centre. Then fold the crown in half the other way and stitch small darts in the same way. This makes the crown look as if it has been made from four pieces and gives it shape. Using strong matching thread work running stitch around the edge of the crown and gently pull up the thread so the leather turns under. Stitch the peak in position with the leather as the right side. To finish, cut a tiny circle of leather and use a single stitch to anchor it to the centre top of the crown where the darts meet to look like a button. Place the cap on the bear and stitch in place.

◆**6** *Making the shoes* Wrap one shoe piece around each foot, stitching the short ends together at the heel. Stitch the lower long edge to the edge of the foot pad using small, even stitches. (Note: if the stitches are too large the leather will pleat but if they are too small the stitch holes will join up and the leather will tear.) The top of the shoes is hidden by the trousers. To make the shoe flaps cut a tiny strip of contrasting leather and fold as shown. Anchor the pleats in place at each end and cut in half. Trim the open ends and stitch one piece to the front of each shoe. Open out the leather and work one stitch on each side through the shoe to hold it in place.

◆**7** *Making the golf club* Use sandpaper to round off the corners of the matchstick. Trim it so it is 2⅓in (6cm) long. Make a strong coffee or tea solution and dip the match into it to tint it brown; leave to dry. Wrap a slither of black insulation tape round one end to form the top of the club and wrap another slither round the match

about ⅛in (3mm) from the other end. For the head of the club make a small ball of brown Fimo or modelling clay. Cut it in half and squash it slightly to shape it. Make small lines across the flat side with a knife and bake it following the manufacturer's instructions (see also step 8). Tape or glue the club head to the match and attach the club to the bear's paw with nylon monofil invisible thread.

◆**8** *Making the golf ball* Roll a piece of white Fimo or modelling clay into a ball and prick it all over with a cocktail stick. Bake it following the manufacturer's instructions. Mount the golfer on a green oval base, and glue the golf ball in position. Finally, bend the bear's limbs to take up the correct pose, ready to swing his club.

TIP – Healthy glow

Try painting your bear's nose with 2 or 3 coats of acrylic varnish or PVA glue to give it a lovely healthy glow.

A GOOD TEAM PLAYER

'Let's all be teddy bears in our next lifetime. Everybody loves them, nobody cares if they're fat and the older they get the more they're worth.'

SHERRI, FROM THE 'BEARLY A PAGE' WEB SITE

When people think of England, especially rural England, there's always cricket on the green. It's as much a part of English life as tea and scones or buckets and spades on the beach. It just wouldn't be cricket not to include this smart young fellow in our set of sports bears.

The bear is 3½in (9cm) tall and based on the pattern for Edmund. He is made from light beige 100% sparse mohair with light contrasting ultra suede paws and inner ears. His legs are made from white fabric and his foot pads are white ultra suede to represent his trousers and shoes. He is also wearing a traditional sleeveless pullover and smart white cap and he has protective shin pads. His bat and the wicket are made from balsa wood which is lightweight and extremely easy to cut.

You will need

- ✤ 6 x 9in (15 x 23cm) piece of light beige 100% sparse mohair
- ✤ Pale ultra suede for paws and inner ears
- ✤ White ultra suede for foot pads
- ✤ Small piece of white upholstery fabric for the legs
- ✤ General-purpose sewing thread to match mohair
- ✤ Black extra-strong nylon thread for attaching eyes
- ✤ Black stranded embroidery thread for the nose
- ✤ Black ultra suede for the nose
- ✤ Darning and fine sharp needles
- ✤ Polyester filling
- ✤ Pair of tiny (2mm) black beads for eyes
- ✤ Small round-nose pliers
- ✤ Long-nose tweezers
- ✤ Four ¼in (6mm) 'T' pin fibreboard cotter pin joints
- ✤ One ¼in (6mm) round pin fibreboard cotter pin joint
- ✤ Galvanised wire

- ✤ Four washer replacements (available from the Great British Bear Company)
- ✤ Stiletto
- ✤ Small teasel brush

For dressing the cricketer
- ✤ Fine white knitted fabric (white pants are ideal!)
- ✤ White felt and thick white thread for shin pads
- ✤ Burgundy stranded embroidery thread
- ✤ Fabric stiffener or a solution 50:50 of PVA glue to water
- ✤ ⅝ x ¼in (15 x 6mm) piece of fine balsa wood for bat
- ✤ Three 1in (2.5cm) lengths of fine balsa wood and one ⅝in (1.5cm) length for the wicket
- ✤ Black insulation tape
- ✤ Clear glue such as Hi-Tack All Purpose Glue
- ✤ Instant-bonding adhesive (Superglue)
- ✤ Black felt-tip pen

Making the cricketer

Trace the pattern pieces for Edmund from page 41 and use them to make card templates (see page 9). Transfer the paws and the front ears from page 65 onto a single layer of ultra suede and cut out, adding an ⅛in (3mm) seam allowance around each piece. Repeat to cut the foot pads from white ultra suede. Transfer the remaining pieces, including the back ears, onto the wrong side of a single layer of light beige 100% sparse mohair with the arrow on the pattern pointing in the direction of the fabric pile. Make sure you transfer the joint position marks onto the two body pieces and the appropriate arms and legs – this is most important. Cut out the pieces, adding an ⅛in (3mm) seam allowance around each one. Make the bear following the instructions below, using backstitch for seams and ladder stitch for closing seams (see page 10).

Making the bear Follow steps 1-11 for Goldie on pages 13–16 to stitch the body, arms, legs and head and to sculpt his eye sockets and add the eyes. To assemble the ears simply place two ear pieces together with right sides facing and raw edges matching and stitch around the curved edge, leaving the straight edge open. Turn right sides out and ladder stitch across the open edge before attaching the ears (see step 12 for Goldie, page 16). To attach the limbs follow steps 2-4 for Amelia on pages 37-38. Fill the body, but not as firmly as the head, then work the nose and mouth following steps 14-16 for Goldie (pages 17-18) but using the photograph opposite as your guide. Brush the bear with a teasel brush to finish.

Dressing the cricketer

Cutting out the pieces Trace the patterns for the pullover, cap and cricket bat given opposite and use them to make card templates. Use your templates to cut the pullover front and back from white stretch-cotton fabric and the cap from white felt. Cut the cricket bat from fine balsa wood.

Making the pullover Neaten the raw edges at the neck, armhole and hem of each piece by turning a tiny (2mm) seam to the wrong side and gluing it in place. When the glue has dried place the two pieces together with shoulder and side seams matching and stitch from A to B and from C to D. Stitch one of the shoulders then turn the pullover right sides out. Using one strand of burgundy embroidery thread work backstitch around the neck and just above the bottom edge of the pullover. Fit the pullover on the bear and close the remaining shoulder seam with ladder stitch.

Making the cap Place two cap pieces together with raw edges matching and stitch one side from A to B. Open out and attach one of the caps to a third piece in the same way. Repeat until all the pieces are stitched together to form the cap. Glue the cap to the peak and leave to dry. When dry use white thread to work tiny blanket stitch all round the cap and peak and then use burgundy thread to backstitch around the cap (see photograph). Glue the small circle of felt on the top of the cap as a button and when dry secure with a small French knot using burgundy embroidery thread. Place the hat on the bear and stitch in position.

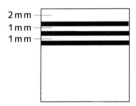

Making the shin pads Cut two 1in (2.5cm) squares of white felt and, starting 2mm below the top of one edge, run thick white thread through the felt so that it is invisible on both sides. Repeat twice more, with 1mm between each row. This creates a raised ridge. Shape the shin pads in the same way as the footballer's pads (see step 2 on page 53); when dry, trim to shape as shown above. Place the shin pads on the bear and use a strand of burgundy embroidery thread to attach it round the back of each leg.

Making the cricket bat Finish the balsa cricket bat by lightly sanding it until the edges are smooth. Then wrap some insulation tape around the handle to give the bear something to grip onto.

Making the wicket Using instant-bonding adhesive stick the three long lengths of balsa wood to the shorter length with one at each end and the third centred in the middle. Mark off the bails above each of the three stumps with black felt-tip pen.

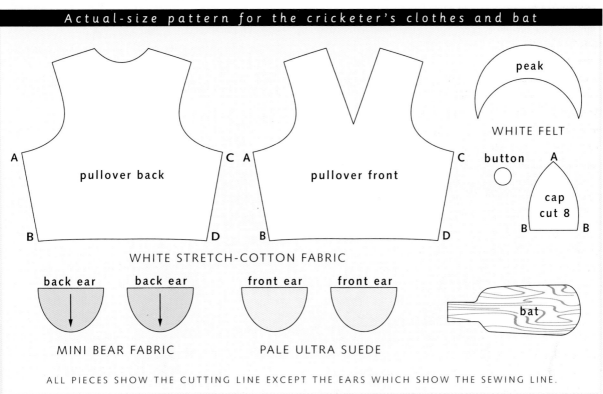

peak

WHITE FELT

button

pullover back

pullover front

A   C A   C A

cap
cut 8

B   D B   D B   B

WHITE STRETCH-COTTON FABRIC

back ear   back ear   front ear   front ear

bat

MINI BEAR FABRIC   PALE ULTRA SUEDE

ALL PIECES SHOW THE CUTTING LINE EXCEPT THE EARS WHICH SHOW THE SEWING LINE.

ON THE PISTE

'The more he looked at it, the more he thought what a brave and clever bear Pooh was, and the more Christopher Robin thought this, the more Pooh looked modestly down his nose and tried to pretend he wasn't.'

FROM 'WINNIE-THE-POOH' BY A. A. MILNE

With his warm red ski outfit and his super skis, poles and goggles, this bear is all set for some serious skiing either on or off piste. He is based on Edmund (see page 40), the boy bear with special limb joints which enable him to participate in active sports like these but his olive long-pile coat and matching ultra suede paws give him quite a different look. He stands approximately 3½in (9cm) tall.

The ski outfit was designed and made by Maggie Spackman of Minikins (see page 95) and features a simple Fair Isle pattern. If you aren't confident knitting a decorative pattern like this, simply make the outfit in a plain colour, following the line count for the pattern but ignoring the colour changes. The sweater is 1½in (4cm) long and 3⅛in (8cm) wide all round with a 1¼in (3cm) side seam; the sleeves are 1⅜in (3.5cm) long.

You will need

- ✛ 6 x 9in (15 x 23cm) piece of long-pile miniature bear upholstery fabric
- ✛ Matching ultra suede for paws and pads
- ✛ General-purpose sewing thread to match bear fabric
- ✛ Extra-strong black nylon thread
- ✛ Black stranded embroidery thread for the nose
- ✛ Black ultra suede for the nose
- ✛ Darning and fine sharp needles
- ✛ Polyester filling
- ✛ Pair of ⅛in (3mm) matching black beads or bear eyes
- ✛ Small round-nose pliers
- ✛ Long-nose tweezers
- ✛ Four ¼in (6mm) 'T' pin fibreboard cotter pin joints
- ✛ One ¼in (6mm) round pin fibreboard cotter pin joint
- ✛ Four washer replacements (available from the Great British Bear Company)

- ✛ Galvanised wire
- ✛ Stiletto
- ✛ Teasel brush

For the clothing and accessories
- ✛ Size 20 needles
- ✛ Safety pins
- ✛ One reel of DMC 80 crochet cotton in the main colour (red)
- ✛ One reel of DMC 80 crochet cotton in a contrasting colour (white)
- ✛ One mini button or bead
- ✛ Fimo or other modelling clay for skis and other accessories in two colours
- ✛ Two cocktail sticks
- ✛ Thin red ribbon
- ✛ Tiny piece of cling film for the goggles

Making the skier

Trace the pattern pieces for Edmund from page 41 and use them to make card templates (see page 9). Transfer the paws and pads onto a single layer of ultra suede and cut out, adding an 1/8in (3mm) seam allowance around each piece. Transfer the remaining pieces onto the wrong side of a single layer of miniature bear fabric with the arrow on the pattern pointing in the direction of the fabric pile. Make sure you transfer the joint position marks onto both the body pieces and the arms and legs – this is most important. Cut out the pieces, adding an 1/8in (3mm) seam allowance around each one. Make the bear in exactly the same way as Edmund (pages 40-41), using backstitch for seams and ladder stitch for closing seams (see page 10).

Knitting the sweater

1 *Knitting the front* Cast on 33 stitches in your main colour (M/C) and work 3 rows in K1 P1 rib. Join on the contrast colour (C/C) and work one row in K1 P1 rib. Then, using M/C, work a further 3 rows in K1 P1 rib, ending on the wrong side. Referring to the chart below, work all six rows of the Fair Isle pattern. Then repeat the

ABBREVIATIONS

C/C = contrast colour   St = stitch
K = knit   St/st = stocking stitch
M/C = main colour   Tog = together
P = pearl   Yfwd = bring the yarn forward

FAIR ISLE PATTERN

Row 1: *(M/C) K3 (C/C) K1 * repeat *to* until last stitch (M/C) K1.
Row 2: *(C/C) P3 (M/C) P1* repeat *to* until last stitch (C/C) P1.
Row 3: *(M/C) K3 (C/C) K1* repeat *to* until last stitch (M/C) K1.
Row 4: *(C/C) P3 (M/C) P1* repeat *to* until last stitch (M/C) P1.
Row 5: *(C/C) K3 (M/C) K1* repeat *to* until last stitch (C/C) K1.
Row 6: *(M/C) P3 (C/C) P1* repeat *to* until last stitch (M/C) P1.

first three rows. Break off C/C and purl 1 row. Continue in M/C with st/st until work measures 1 1/4in (3cm), ending on the wrong side **.

2 *Working the armhole* Continuing in st/st, cast off 2 sts at the beginning of the next 2 rows. Decrease 1 st at each end of next and every alternate row until 15 sts remain. Place these remaining sts on a safety pin.

3 *Knitting the back* Work in the same way as the front until **. To work the armhole continue in st/st, casting off 2 sts at the beginning of the next 2 rows. Decrease 1 st at the beginning of the next row and knit 11 sts. Cast off 5 sts and knit the last 2 sts together. K2 tog then purl 1 row. Continue working on this set of stitches. Decrease 1 st at armhole edge of every alternate row until 5 sts remain. Place these 5 sts securely on a safety pin. Now rejoin the thread to the second set of 11 sts and purl 1 row. Work as previously but reverse the shapings to form the armhole.

4 *Working the sleeves* Cast on 33 sts in M/C. Work 2 rows K1 P1 rib then change to C/C and work 1 row rib. Rejoin M/C and work a further 2 rows rib. Continue in st/st, working the first two rows of the Fair Isle pattern given in the chart. Work the next row as follows: *(C/C) increase 1 stitch *(M/C) K3 (C/C) K1* repeat * to * to last stitch (M/C) K1 and increase 1. Break off C/C and continue in st/st, increasing at each end of the 7th row (37 sts). Now work 13 rows in st/st (20 rows worked in all). Cast off 2 sts at the beginning of the next 2 rows. Decrease 1 st at each end of every row until 7 sts remain, finishing on the wrong side. Work 3 rows straight. Put the remaining 7 sts on a safety pin and work another sleeve in the same way.

5 *Working the over wrap* Using M/C pick up and knit the 5 sts cast off at the back opening. Slip 1, K1, P1, K2. On the next row slip 1, P1, K1, P1, K1. Work 5 more rows in straight rib. With the right side facing slip these 5 sts onto the same safety pin as the right-hand side back.

6 *Working the under wrap* Cast on 5 sts. Slip 1, K1, P1, K2. On the next row slip 1, P1, K1, P1, K1. Using these 2 rows work 9 rows in rib.

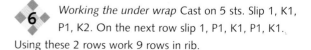

7 *Working the neck* With right side facing. Pick up and knit 5 sts of the left back, then pick up and knit 7 sts of the sleeve. Pick up and knit 15 sts of the front, then pick up and knit 7 sts of the remaining sleeve. Finally, pick up and knit 10 sts of right back and over wrap (49 sts). Slip 1, P1, K1, P1, K1 (P1, P2 tog) * repeat 12 times. P1, K1, P1, K2. Turn and rib to the end. Join on C/C slip 1, P1, K1, yfwd, K2 tog (to form a buttonhole). Rejoin M/C and rib to the end. Cast off in rib.

8 *Making up the sweater* First join the raglan seams. Next join the side and sleeve seams. Slipstitch the over wrap to the side of the neck opening. Slipstitch the under wrap to the side of the neck opening and stitch the bottom edge in position behind the over wrap. Sew a mini button or bead onto the under wrap to correspond with the buttonhole.

Knitting the ski hat

1 *Knitting the hat* Cast on 33 sts in M/C. Work 4 rows K1 P1 rib then join on C/C and work 2 rows rib. Rejoin M/C and work a further 4 rows rib. Work 20 rows straight st/st then work 3 rows in the Fair Isle pattern given on the previous page. Purl 1 row. Knit 3 rows. Purl 1 row. Work 3 rows in the Fair Isle pattern. Now work 20 rows straight st/st and then rib 4 rows. Join on C/C and work 2 rows rib. Rejoin M/C and work a further 4 rows rib. Cast off in rib.

2 *Making up the hat* Fold the hat in half widthways so the knit row runs along the top of the hat. Stitch the side seams to the ribbing. Turn right-side out and stitch the ribbing then turn back the ribbing to form a cuff. In each corner of the hat take lengths of M/C and C/C thread and fasten several over-sewn loops. Snip the ends of the loops to form small tassels.

Knitting the scarf

1 *Working the knitting* Cast on 10 sts in M/C. Work 10 rows in slip 1 K1 P1 rib. Join in C/C for 4 rows. Rejoin M/C and continue in rib until work measures 4in (10cm). Work 4 rows in C/C then work 10 rows in M/C. Cast off in rib.

2 *Completing the scarf* Run a thread through the ends of the scarf and draw into a gather. Fasten off. At the ends make several fastened loops in the same way as for the hat tassels (see step 2 above) and trim neatly. This gives the scarf a fringe.

Making the accessories

1 *Making the skis and poles* Cut the end off the two cocktail sticks so they are 2$\frac{1}{4}$in (6cm) long and dip them in a solution of strong black coffee to colour them slightly. To make the skis roll out a long piece of Fimo or other modelling clay and cut out two pieces 3$\frac{1}{4}$ x $\frac{1}{2}$in (8.5 x 1cm). Round off the front of both skis and curl the end up slightly. Decorate the skis with a contrasting colour and use a large needle or stiletto to make two holes, side by side, halfway along each ski so you can attach them to the bear. Using pale Fimo or other modelling clay cut out two tiny circles approximately $\frac{1}{2}$in (1cm) in diameter. Using a cocktail stick make a hole through the centre of each, then wrap the blunt end of each cocktail stick with more pale Fimo.

2 *Making the goggles* Fold a small piece of cling film several times and then cut out the goggle pattern given here. Carefully roll out a long, thin piece of Fimo and lay it on top of the cling film following the shape of the goggles. Make a tiny loop on each side so they can be attached to the bear. Lay the goggles over a skewer to give the curved shape and bake, together with the other Fimo items, following the instructions given on the packet.

goggles

3 *Assembling the accessories* To make the poles carefully push a Fimo circle onto the pointed end of each cocktail stick. Use a tiny dab of glue, if required, to hold in place. Sew a loop of ribbon to the top of each ski pole and loop round the bear's paw. Attach the goggles to the bear using a piece of the same ribbon, anchoring it in place with small stitches, if required. Wrap a short length of ribbon round each foot and stitch in place, then stitch the skis to the bear using the holes you made in the skis before baking. Bend the limbs as required and your bear is all ready to go.

GONE FISHING

'Even Paddington had a go over the stern with a piece of string and a bent pin which Mrs Bird found in her handbag.'

FROM 'PADDINGTON ABROAD' BY MICHAEL BOND

So many people like to escape from their busy lives with a packed lunch and bag of fishing tackle to enjoy the tranquillity of the waterside, and bears are no exception. Paddington bear had only a piece of string and a bent pin to fish with, but this young sportsman has all the right equipment for a spot of fly fishing, including a net, green boots, fishing waistcoat and hat. He even has a comfortable stool to sit on.

He is made using the same pattern as for Edmund but in mink-brown upholstery fabric and he has contrasting ultra suede paws and pads. His hat and fishing waistcoat are made from ultra suede and his legs are cut from checked upholstery fabric to look like trousers. He has armature in all four limbs to enable him to take up many poses, but if you prefer you can put standard joints in either his arms or his legs or both.

You will need

- 6 x 9in (15 x 23cm) mink-brown miniature bear upholstery fabric
- Contrasting ultra suede for paws and pads
- Tiny checked upholstery fabric for legs/trousers
- General-purpose sewing thread to match bear fabric
- Black extra-strong nylon thread for attaching the eyes
- Black stranded embroidery thread for the nose
- Black ultra suede for the nose
- Darning and fine sharp needles
- Polyester filling
- Pair of ⅛in (3mm) black beads for eyes
- Small round-nose pliers
- Long-nose tweezers
- Four ¼in (6mm) 'T' pin fibreboard cotter pin joints
- One ¼in (6mm) round pin fibreboard cotter pin joint
- Four washer replacements (available from the Great British Bear Company)
- Galvanised wire

- Stiletto
- Small teasel brush

For dressing the fishing bear
- Light beige ultra suede
- Small piece of contrasting ultra suede
- Fabric for the stool seat
- Two tiny buttons for the waistcoat back
- Feather for the hat
- Fine balsa wood for the rod, net handle and stool
- Two ⅜in (10mm) diameter pearl-coloured buttons with shank
- 30 amp fuse wire
- Metallic thread for the fishing line
- Fine black net for the fishing net
- Black insulation tape or woven tape
- Fine (2.5mm) copper wire
- Green Fimo or modelling clay for the boots
- Instant bonding adhesive

Making the fishing bear

Trace the pattern pieces for Edmund from page 41 and use them to make card templates (see page 9). Transfer the paws and pads onto a single layer of ultra suede and cut out, adding an ⅛in (3mm) seam allowance around each piece. Transfer the legs on to checked fabric and remaining pieces onto the wrong side of a single layer of miniature bear fabric with the arrow on the pattern pointing in the direction of the fabric pile. Make sure you transfer the joint position marks onto the two body pieces and the appropriate arms and legs. Cut out, adding an ⅛in (3mm) seam allowance around each one. Make the bear following the instructions for Edmund on pages 40-41, using backstitch for seams and ladder stitch for closing seams (see page 10).

Dressing the fishing bear

1 *Cutting out the pieces* Trace the patterns for the waistcoat and hat on page 72 and use them to make card templates. Fold the light beige ultra suede in half and cut the waistcoat, placing it on the fold as indicated. Unfold the ultra suede and cut out the hat pieces. Cut the pocket sections and belt casing from contrasting ultra suede.

2 *Making the waistcoat* With right sides facing fold the waistcoat to match adjacent side edges AB and stitch both side seams. Use running stitch to sew the two large patch pockets to the front parallel with the bottom of the waistcoat. Sew the top pocket on the right-hand side and the pocket flap on the left-hand side so the top edges of the top pocket and pocket flap are level. Across the centre back of the waistcoat work running stitch for ⅜in (1cm). Gently pull up the stitching to shape the jacket and stitch the belt casing on top. Attach a button at each end to finish then fit the waistcoat on the bear.

3 *Making the hat* With right sides facing match two crown pieces together. Stitch one side seam from A to B then open out the pieces. Continue stitching crown pieces together in the same way until all the side edges are joined. Turn right sides out and lay the brim of the hat over

the crown. Stitch it in place, then lay the hat band over the top and sew it on with tiny stitches. Fit the hat on the bear and anchor it in position with a few stitches. Finally, tuck a tiny piece of feather under the hat band.

4 *Making the fishing rod* (shown overleaf) Bend the fuse wire to make three eyelets. Cut a narrow 3½in (9cm) length of balsa wood and slide the three eyelets

TIP – Small-scale fabric designs

If you have trouble finding fabric for your bear's clothing, try contacting dolls' house manufacturers or take a look in your nearest patchwork shop. Both stock fabrics with suitably small designs.

Actual-size pattern for the fishing bear's clothes

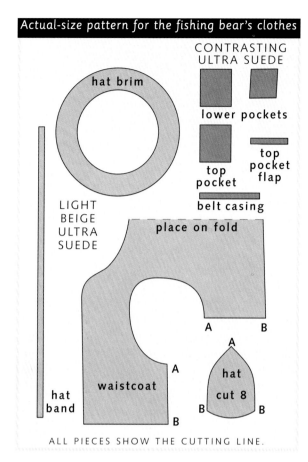

CONTRASTING ULTRA SUEDE

hat brim

lower pockets

top pocket flap

top pocket

LIGHT BEIGE ULTRA SUEDE

belt casing

place on fold

A   B

A

hat cut 8

A

hat band   waistcoat

B   B

B

ALL PIECES SHOW THE CUTTING LINE.

eyelet

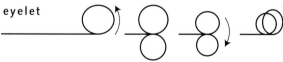

onto it, positioning one at the end and the other two spaced 1¹⁄₄in (3cm) apart; glue them in place. For the reel use instant-bonding adhesive to stick one pearl button to the side of the rod at the end without the eyelet. Thread an 8in (20cm) length of metallic thread through the button shank

hook

and all three eyelets. Now make a hook with fuse wire to tie onto the end, as shown above. To finish, cut the shank off the second pearl button and glue it opposite the first one.

5 *Making the net* Cut a 1¹⁄₂in (4cm) length of balsa wood for the handle and a 4in (10cm) length of copper wire for the net top. Bend the wire round a tube

1in (2.5cm) in diameter to make a circle, then attach the excess wire to the end of the net handle with black insulation tape. Next cut a 1¹⁄₄ x 2¹⁄₂in (3 x 6cm) piece of net and use black thread to slipstitch it to the copper wire. Do not cut off the thread at the end but continue to stitch down the side of the net to join the edges, then stitch across the bottom.

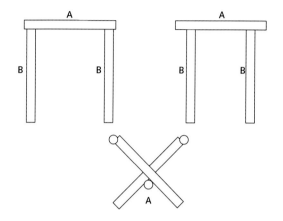

6 *Constructing the stool* Cut three 1¹⁄₄in (3cm) lengths of fine balsa wood (A) and four 1in (2.5cm) lengths (B). Use instant-bonding adhesive to glue one leg (B) to each end of one rail (A) at right angles, as shown above left. Glue the other two legs (B) to a second rail (A) a little way in from each end (above right). When the glue is dry cross the two sections over and glue the remaining piece, A, under the cross to join the sections, as shown. Apply glue to the edges of each top rail and stick the fabric on, folding it round to the underside. When the stool is open the fabric should be taut.

7 *Making the boots* Use green Fimo or modelling clay to make a pair of green wellington boots to stand next to the bear. Bake them following the manufacturer's instructions.

GAME, SET
AND MATCH

'A good arctophile knows bears apart like a shepherd knows his sheep.'

MARY HILDESLEY

This tennis champion is the most flexible of all the bears, and she needs to be to stay at the top of her sport. In addition to full armature in her limbs she has a double neck joint so she can keep her eye on the ball.

The tennis player is made from the same pattern as Amelia but from soft pink miniature bear upholstery fabric with matching paws and pads. She wears a pretty white tennis dress with pink and white trim and has a visor to keep the sun out of her eyes. She even sports realistic sweatbands. Her racket is made from white wire, thread and tape and her ball is made from modelling clay.

You will need

- 6 x 9in (15 x 23cm) piece of pink miniature bear upholstery fabric
- Matching ultra suede for paws and pads
- General-purpose sewing thread to match the bear fabric
- Black extra-strong nylon thread for attaching eyes
- Black stranded embroidery thread for the nose
- Black ultra suede for the nose
- Darning and fine sharp needles
- Polyester filling
- Pair of tiny (2mm) black beads for eyes
- Small round-nose pliers
- Long-nose tweezers
- Four ¼in (6mm) 'T' pin fibreboard cotter pin joints
- Two ¼in fibreboard discs and two round-end cotter pins

- Galvanised wire and four washer replacements (available from the Great British Bear Company)
- Stiletto
- Small teasel brush

For dressing the tennis player
- White cotton fabric
- Pale pink picot trim
- Narrow white braid
- 2 x 1in (5 x 2.5cm) piece of white felt
- Fine white wire
- White insulation tape or woven tape
- Fabric stiffener or a 50:50 solution of PVA glue to water
- Strong glue
- White Fimo or modelling clay

Making the tennis player

Trace the pattern pieces for Amelia from page 39 and use them to make card templates (see page 9). Transfer the paws and pads onto a single layer of ultra suede and cut out, adding an ⅛in (3mm) seam allowance around each piece. Transfer the remaining pieces onto the wrong side of a single layer of pink miniature bear upholstery fabric with the arrow on the pattern pointing in the direction of the fabric pile. Make sure you transfer the joint position marks onto the two body pieces and the appropriate arms and legs – this is most important. Cut out the pieces, adding an ⅛in (3mm) seam allowance around each one. Make the bear following the instructions below, using backstitch for seams and ladder stitch for closing seams (see page 10).

1 *Getting started* Follow steps 1-9 for Goldie on pages 13-16 to join the body pieces, stitch the arms and legs, make the head and add the eyes. Using a double length of extra-strong nylon thread, work running stitch around the head opening. Now hook one round-end cotter pin through the other. Place a

fibreboard disc on one pin and use small round-nose pliers to turn the prongs back onto the disc, as shown. Place the part with the turned-back cotter pin into the bear's head and pull the running stitch tight so the opening is

completely closed with just the joint pin protruding. Secure the thread and finish by working several extra stitches around the pin. Cut off the excess thread.

2 *Finishing the neck joint* Insert the ends of the cotter pin joint through the body at the point indicated on the pattern. Through the body opening, peel the fabric back so the pin ends are accessible and 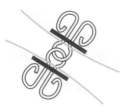 put on the other washer. Open out the two prongs of the pin and curl each one round, back onto the washer, as shown.

3 *Completing the bear* Make and attach the bear's ears following step 12 for Goldie (page 16), then attach the limbs following steps 2-4 for Amelia (pages 37-38). Fill the body, but not as firmly as the head, then work the nose and mouth following steps 15-16 for Goldie (pages 17-18). Cut a narrow strip of pink upholstery fabric and use it to cover the neck joint. Stitch the ends together at the back of the bear. Finally, brush the bear with a teasel brush.

Dressing the tennis player

1 *Making the dress* Cut the four dress pieces given right from white cotton fabric, making sure you place each one on a fold of the fabric as indicated. Pin two dress pieces together with right sides facing and raw edges matching and stitch from A all round the dress to B, leaving a small gap for turning. Turn right sides out and close the gap with ladder stitch. Press well with an iron. Repeat to join the other two dress pieces. Now lay the joined pieces together with edges matching and ladder stitch the shoulders together (this avoids bulk at the seam). Ladder stitch one side seam in the same way. Attach the pink picot trim close to the bottom of the dress, starting at the open side seam and leaving the end of the braid extending slightly past the edge of the fabric. Fit the dress on the bear and ladder stitch the final side seam, enclosing the raw ends of the picot trim for a neat finish.

2 *Adding the visor* Soak the felt in fabric stiffener or glue solution and leave to dry, then cut the visor pattern given right from the felt. Fit the visor on the bear's head and stitch in place, then stick a piece of white braid around the back of the head from one end of the visor to the other, tucking the raw ends under. Attach a piece of white trim around each wrist too for sweatbands.

3 *Making the racket* Twist two lengths of fine wire together and bend them into the shape of a tennis racket. Glue white cotton thread across the racket from top to bottom, sticking it in place at each end. Weave cotton thread across the racket, going under and over the vertical threads, and again stick it in place. Leave to dry. Finally, trim the length of the handle as required and wrap it with white insulation tape.

4 *Completing the look* Roll out a small ball of white Fimo or modelling clay and bake it following the manufacturer's instructions. Glue the ball to one of the bear's paws and stitch the tennis racket to the other paw. Pose the bear in a serving position to show real movement. The posed bear may need a little support, so make a base and attach the bear with pins from the bottom of the base (see page 47).

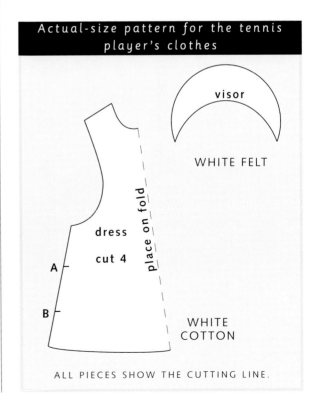

Actual-size pattern for the tennis player's clothes

visor

WHITE FELT

dress

cut 4

place on fold

A

B

WHITE COTTON

ALL PIECES SHOW THE CUTTING LINE.

NURSERY SCENE

A miniature bear with her miniature companions

After the kind of day which leaves a bear exhausted, perhaps engaging in one of her many favourite activities, it's off to bed for our bear for the type of long, deep sleep which bears do best. But does a bear go to bed on her own? No, she certainly does not. She has her own pint-sized companions which you can make to go with her. Of course, she has her own tiny teddy bears and our bear also has a friendly Scottie dog, a duck, a grey lop-eared rabbit and a pretty rag doll. All of these are simple to make, particularly once you have mastered the basics of bear-making.

If you decide to make the bear with all her companions you may like to present her in a setting. All the characters are designed to fit in with the ½ scale used in dolls' house manufacture so you can make and fit a box room using dolls' house furniture or even take over a whole dolls' house. The painted furniture and tiny toys shown here are all made by specialists but if you are good with wood or paper and card you can try making your own furniture. You'll find a wonderful source of inspiration, advice and even patterns for suitable designs in dolls' house magazines.

BEDTIME BEAR

'People believe in teddy bears because teddy bears believe in people.'

UNKNOWN

This cuddly bear is wearing a cosy dressing gown made from luxurious silk chenille and a co-ordinating nightcap to keep out the draughts. She clutches her hot-water bottle tightly to keep her snug even on the coldest night and is obviously just off to bed where her toys will keep her company all night long. She is made from the same pattern as William, the graduation bear (page 24), but a change of fabric and the addition of her clothing give her a whole new look. Make her from mid-brown miniature bear fabric as shown, or select a more colourful fabric if you prefer.

FINISHED SIZE
3½IN (9CM)

You will need

- 6 x 9in (15 x 23cm) piece of miniature bear fabric (American upholstery fabric, short-pile mohair or soft upholstery fabric)
- Matching ultra suede for paws and pads
- General-purpose sewing thread to match the bear fabric
- Extra-strong black nylon thread
- Black stranded embroidery thread for the nose
- Black ultra suede for the nose
- Darning and fine sharp needles
- Polyester filling
- Pair of tiny (2mm) black beads or bear eyes
- One ¼in (6mm) round pin fibreboard cotter pin joint
- Small teasel brush

For trimming and accessorising Bedtime Bear

- Silk chenille or other soft fabric for the dressing gown
- Matching thread
- Stranded embroidery thread for the dressing gown cord, ideally in three different colours
- Ultra suede for the hot-water bottle
- Pale cotton fabric for a nightcap
- Nylon monofil thread (invisible thread)

Making Bedtime Bear

Trace the pattern pieces for William from page 26 and use them to make card templates (see page 9). Transfer the paws and pads onto a single layer of ultra suede and cut out, adding an ⅛in (3mm) seam allowance around each piece. Transfer the remaining pieces onto the wrong side of a single layer of miniature bear fabric with the arrow on the pattern pointing in the direction of the fabric pile. Cut out the pieces, adding an ⅛in (3mm) seam allowance around each one. Make the bear following the instructions given for William on page 25, using backstitch for seams and ladder stitch for closing seams (see page 10).

Dressing and accessorising Bedtime Bear

1 *Cutting out the pieces* Trace the patterns for the dressing gown, nightcap and hot-water bottle given overleaf and use them to make templates. Fold the chenille fabric in half and cut the main dressing gown piece, placing the centre back edge on the fold as indicated on the pattern. Unfold the fabric and cut the two sleeves. Cut the nightcap from pale, soft fabric and the hot-water bottle pieces from ultra suede.

2 *Stitching the dressing gown* Fold the body of the dressing gown with right sides facing so the adjacent seams AB match. Stitch these seams. Take each sleeve piece and turn ⅛in (3mm) onto the wrong side along the long straight edge and stitch in place. Then fold each sleeve in half with right sides facing to match the short straight edges and stitch the seam from E to F. Turn the sleeve right side out. Work a small running stitch around the top of the sleeve between G and G but do not finish off the thread.

3 *Finishing the dressing gown* Insert the sleeve into the dressing gown by matching the side seam and the sleeve seam. Pull up the running stitch and ease the top of the sleeve to fit into the armhole. Backstitch in place. Repeat with the other sleeve. Turn a small hem around the bottom of the dressing gown and stitch in place, then neaten the front of the dressing gown by turning the edge under and stitching in place – go all round the neck and both fronts. Fit the dressing gown onto the bear and randomly stitch any loose fabric in place.

4 *Making the dressing-gown cord* Take six strands of stranded embroidery thread (ideally two each of three different colours). Knot all six strands together at one end and pin the knot to a pin cushion, as shown. Twist the six strands together until they start to curl up. Take the knot from the pin cushion and fold the twisted threads in half. Shake the threads and they should all twist together into one cord. Knot the two ends together. Cut the

TIP – Adding claws

If you like you can give Bedtime Bear – or any of the other bears in this book – some claws. Simply follow the instructions given for Hugo, step 7 on page 46.

cord to the correct length and tie a knot to stop it from unwinding. Tie it round the bear's waist and trim the two ends, then fray back to the knots so they look like tassels.

5 *Stitching the nightcap* Fold ½in (1cm) to the right side along the long straight edge of the nightcap. With the folded-over edge inside, fold the cap in half lengthways

and stitch the seam from the fold to the point. Turn right-side out. Make a small pompon by rolling up a ball of polyester filling and stitching through it with white thread; attach it to the point of the cap. Place the nightcap on the bear's head and stitch in place using nylon monofil invisible thread.

6 *Making the hot-water bottle* Place one hot-water bottle piece on top of the other and topstitch together all round, using tiny stitches and leaving the top open. Insert a very small amount of polyester filling through the hole in the top to give the hot-water bottle some shape and stitch across the neck to enclose it. Insert two tiny pieces of ultra suede into the actual neck of the hot-water bottle to fill it out. (If you used white polyester filling for this it would show.) Attach the hot-water bottle to the bear's paw.

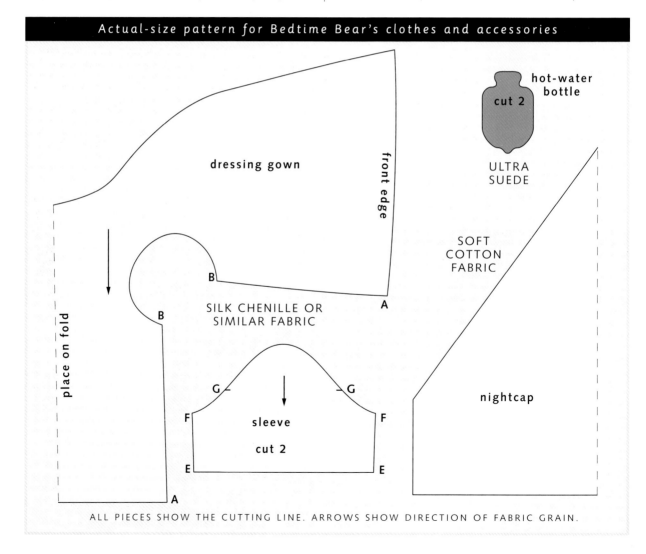

Actual-size pattern for Bedtime Bear's clothes and accessories

dressing gown

front edge

place on fold

SILK CHENILLE OR SIMILAR FABRIC

hot-water bottle

cut 2

ULTRA SUEDE

SOFT COTTON FABRIC

nightcap

sleeve

cut 2

ALL PIECES SHOW THE CUTTING LINE. ARROWS SHOW DIRECTION OF FABRIC GRAIN.

SCOTTIE DOG

The Bedtime Bear has a little black Scottie dog who shares the nursery and helps to keep the smaller toys in order. At just 1in (2.5cm) tall he is the same height as Tiny Ted (see page 90), the Bedtime Bear's smallest teddy, but his courage and confidence ensure that he gets his way. He is made from short-pile black miniature bear fabric with tiny black seed beads for eyes and he sports a flamboyant bow tie which helps ensure that he gets noticed.

FINISHED SIZE
1IN (2.5CM)

You will need

+ 6 x 4in (15 x 10cm) piece of black upholstery fabric
+ Black general-purpose sewing thread
+ Extra-strong black nylon thread
+ Dark grey embroidery thread for the nose
+ Polyester filling
+ Pair of matching black seed beads for eyes
+ Clear nail polish or Fray Check
+ Small, sharp pointed scissors
+ Narrow red ribbon

Making the Scottie dog

Trace the pattern pieces for the Scottie dog from page 82 and use them to make card templates (see page 9). Transfer the pieces to a single layer of miniature bear fabric with the arrow on the pattern pointing in the direction of the fabric pile and cut them out, adding an ⅛in (3mm) seam allowance around each one. Make the dog following the instructions below, using backstitch for seams and ladder stitch for closing seams (see page 10).

 Attaching the head gusset With right sides facing pin one body piece to the head gusset, matching points A and B, and stitch from A to B around one side of the head gusset. Repeat to attach the other body piece to the other side of the head gusset. When you reach B continue stitching the two body pieces together round to C.

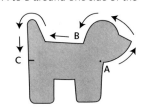

 Completing the body With right sides facing pin the body gusset to one body piece, matching the lower edges. Sew from A under the chin right round the body gusset to C, then continue stitching to join on the other body piece to the body gusset, stitching from C round to A.

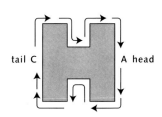

3 *Stuffing the dog* You will need to cut a slit in the dog so you can turn him out and stuff him. First draw a line down the centre of the body gusset with clear nail polish or Fray Check and allow to dry well. Then cut a slit down the centre of the body gusset, where you applied the nail polish or Fray Check, using small sharp-pointed scissors. Turn the dog right sides out and stuff him but do not close the seam yet. Attach the seed bead eyes in the same way as for Goldie, step 9 (page 16) and close the split in the dog's tummy with ladder stitch.

4 *Adding the ears* Fold each ear in half with right sides facing and stitch round the semi-circle, leaving the thread attached. Cut along the fold and turn right sides out. Ladder stitch along the opening. Now fold the ear in half and stitch the two corners together, still leaving the thread attached. Pin the ears on the head and check they look well balanced then attach them using ladder stitch.

5 *Completing the dog* Using one strand of dark grey embroidery thread stitch the nose in the shape of a V using small satin stitches. Then stitch the mouth in the same way as for Goldie, step 16 (page 18). Now sculpt the legs. Using extra-strong black nylon thread with a knot in the end come out at the top side of the front leg and insert your needle back in exactly the same hole as you came out of, taking your needle straight across the body and coming out at the top front of the other leg, in the same way as when thread jointing a bear (see step 4, page 25). Repeat this once more and gently pull tight to draw the legs in. Finish off the thread and repeat this process with the back legs. Add the finishing touch by tying a red ribbon round the dog's neck.

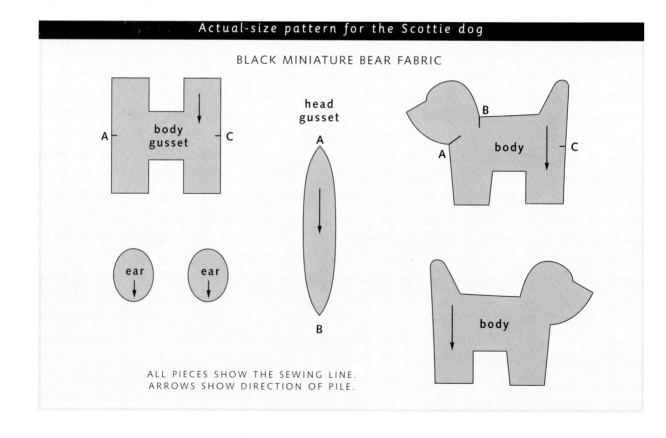

Actual-size pattern for the Scottie dog

BLACK MINIATURE BEAR FABRIC

body gusset

head gusset

ear

ear

body

body

ALL PIECES SHOW THE SEWING LINE.
ARROWS SHOW DIRECTION OF PILE.

MINI DUCK

Farm animals are always popular with children and most have a particular soft spot for ducks. These friendly and entertaining birds are constantly cheerful and fascinating to watch as they waddle comically about on the grass or swim vigorously on the water.

This duck is made from felt which is particularly easy to work with. His body is yellow and he has an orange beak and feet – one of the most traditional duck combinations. His head is jointed so he can look around at the other toys in the nursery with his beady eyes and he wears an optional bow tie.

You will need

- 4 x 5in (10 x 13cm) piece of yellow felt
- 2in (5cm) square of orange felt
- Lightweight iron-on interfacing
- General-purpose sewing thread to match the felt
- Fusible bonding fabric such as Bondaweb
- Orange stranded embroidery thread, slightly darker than the felt
- Pair of black matching seed beads for eyes
- One metal $^{1}/_{4}$in (6mm) cotter pin joint (finer than fibreboard)
- Polyester filling
- Narrow ribbon for trimming the duck

FINISHED SIZE
1IN (2.5CM)

Making the duck

Trace the pattern pieces for Mini Duck from page 84 and use them to make card templates (see page 9). Transfer the beak pattern onto orange felt and cut out, adding an $^{1}/_{8}$in (3mm) seam allowance all round. Cut the remaining orange felt into two and fuse the pieces together with bonding fabric, following the manufacturer's instructions. Using the templates for the feet as a guide, cut out the feet from the bonded felt without adding a seam allowance – do not transfer the cutting line to the felt as it will leave a black line that will show. Bond two pieces of yellow felt together and cut the wings in the same way. Now iron some lightweight iron-on interfacing onto yellow felt. Transfer the remaining pieces onto a single layer of the interfaced felt and cut out, adding an $^{1}/_{8}$in (3mm) seam allowance all round. Make the duck following the instructions below, using backstitch for seams and ladder stitch for closing seams (see page 10).

Actual-size pattern for the duck

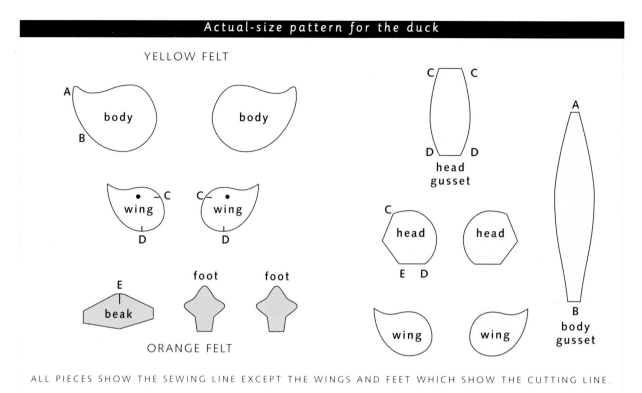

YELLOW FELT

ORANGE FELT

ALL PIECES SHOW THE SEWING LINE EXCEPT THE WINGS AND FEET WHICH SHOW THE CUTTING LINE.

1 *Joining the body* With right sides together align the body gusset at A with one body piece at A and backstitch from A to B. Repeat to attach the other body piece to the other side of the body gusset. Finish off the thread and turn the body right sides out. Now take the head gusset and put it right sides together with one head piece, matching the pieces at C and D; backstitch from C to D. Starting with a new piece of thread return to C and attach the other head piece to the other side of the head gusset in the same way.

2 *Completing the body* Align the centre of the beak (opposite E) with the centre of the head gusset and backstitch it in place. Complete the head by stitching from the tip of the beak at E down to F on the head. Turn right sides out and fill the head. Attach the eyes to the side of the head following the instructions for Goldie, step 9 (page 16), then prepare the head joint and attach the head in the same way as for Goldie, steps 10-11. Make a hole with a stiletto in the body for the cotter pin to go through and finish the neck joint inside the body cavity. Fill the body and close the opening with ladder stitch.

3 *Adding the wings and feet* Using one strand of orange embroidery thread work buttonhole stitch around the wings and feet. Position the wings on the body and attach by stitching from C to D with ladder stitch. Position the feet and attach them with ladder stitch too.

4 *Outlining the eyes* Using one strand of orange embroidery thread outline the eyes with a detached chain stitch as follows. Bring your needle out at the front of the eye, close to the bead. Insert the needle back into the same hole it came out of and bring it out at the other side of the bead. Before pulling through, wrap the thread round the needle as shown. Gently pull the thread and insert the needle next to the point where it came out, anchoring the loop down. Repeat with the other eye and finish off the thread. Tie a ribbon round the duck's neck, if desired.

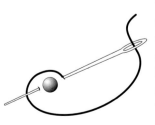

LOP-EARED RABBIT

With his tiny round pink nose, long whiskers and twinkling beady eyes, this little grey rabbit is bound to appeal to the very young. He's sitting up in the inquisitive position often adopted by rabbits and is obviously eager to join in all the fun. Rabbit is probably at the bottom of the nursery pecking order along with Mini Duck, but Bedtime Bear loves him just as much as all the others.

Making the rabbit

Trace the pattern pieces for the rabbit from page 86 and use them to make card templates (see page 9). Transfer the inner ears onto pink ultra suede and cut out, adding an ⅛in (3mm) seam allowance all round. Transfer the remaining pieces onto the wrong side of a single layer of miniature bear fabric with the arrow on the pattern pointing in the direction of the fabric pile. (Remember to use white fabric for the tail.) Cut out the pieces, adding an ⅛in (3mm) seam allowance around each one. Make the rabbit following the instructions below, using backstitch for seams and ladder stitch for closing seams (see page 10).

You will need

- ÷ 8 x 4in (20 x 10cm) piece of light grey miniature bear upholstery fabric
- ÷ Soft white upholstery fabric for the tail
- ÷ Pink ultra suede for the inner ears
- ÷ General-purpose sewing thread to match the main fabric
- ÷ White general-purpose sewing thread
- ÷ Extra-strong nylon thread for jointing
- ÷ Pink embroidery thread for the nose
- ÷ Horsehair or nylon thread for the whiskers
- ÷ Polyester filling
- ÷ Pair of matching black seed beads for eyes
- ÷ One ¼in (6mm) metal cotter pin joint (finer than fibreboard)
- ÷ Narrow ribbon for trimming the rabbit
- ÷ Strong glue

FINISHED SIZE
1¼IN (4CM)

1 *Joining the body* Match the body gusset to one body piece at A and B and stitch together with right sides facing and raw edges matching. Match the second body piece to the other side of the gusset at C and B and stitch in the same way. With right sides together now stitch the body pieces together from D to E, and then F to B. Turn right sides out.

2 *Making and attaching the head* Join the head pieces, attach the gusset and stuff the head in the same way as for Goldie, steps 5-7 (page 14). Add the eyes following step 9 for Goldie, then prepare the head joint following step 10. Now use extra-strong thread to work running stitch around the neck opening of the body. Insert the cotter pin joint with the head attached and put on the other washer. Open out the two prongs of the pin and curl each one round, back onto the washer. Finally, stuff the rabbit and close the back seam with ladder stitch.

3 *Making the ears* Pin a pink inner ear to each outer ear with right sides facing and raw edges matching and stitch together around the curved sides and top, leaving the straight edge open. Turn right sides out and ladder stitch across the open edge.

4 *Finishing the rabbit* Using a single strand of pink embroidery thread work a small round nose and a small mouth (see steps 15-16, pages 17-18). Line up the ears with the head gusset seams and ladder stitch in place, then fold the ears down and anchor them to the head. Using a double length of white thread work running stitch around the tail circle. Insert a tiny piece of stuffing and gently pull up the running stitch thread to form a ball. Secure the thread and ladder stitch the tail in position with the raw edges facing the rabbit's body.

5 *Adding the whiskers* Thread your needle with a strand of horsehair or nylon thread and insert it just beside the nose, bringing it out on the other side. Repeat until you have sufficient whiskers, leaving them all at different lengths to add character. Use a cocktail stick to put a tiny dab of glue on each one to stop it from coming out. Finish the rabbit with a bow round his neck.

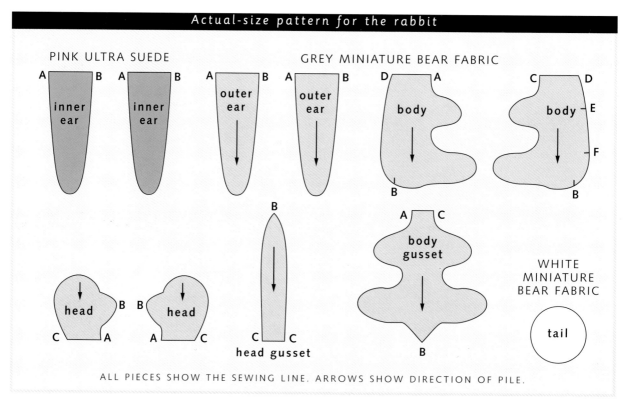

Actual-size pattern for the rabbit

PINK ULTRA SUEDE

GREY MINIATURE BEAR FABRIC

inner ear

inner ear

outer ear

outer ear

body

body

head

head

head gusset

body gusset

WHITE MINIATURE BEAR FABRIC

tail

ALL PIECES SHOW THE SEWING LINE. ARROWS SHOW DIRECTION OF PILE.

RAG DOLL

Every little girl's nursery needs at least one doll, and the Bedtime Bear's room is no exception. This pretty rag doll will listen to Bedtime Bear's secrets, hear her worries and fears and play with her when she's alone.

Although she is just 2in (5cm) tall and made from only one pattern piece the rag doll is extremely convincing and has all the characteristics of a larger and more complicated doll. This is achieved by stitching across the tops of the limbs and tying up the wrists and neck to give added shape. The dolls' lovely long hair is made from stranded embroidery thread and her beautiful dress is simply made from short lengths of ribbon.

FINISHED SIZE
2IN (5CM)

You will need

* 6 x 4in (15 x 10cm) off-white cotton or fine calico
* 4in (10cm) length of ⅝in (1.5cm) wide cream ribbon for the underskirt
* 6½in (16.5cm) length of ⅝in (1.5cm) wide yellow satin ribbon for the dress
* Short length of matching braid or narrow ribbon
* Polyester filling
* Brown stranded embroidery thread for the hair
* Stranded embroidery thread to stitch the face – black or navy blue for the eyes, light pink for the nose, red for the lips and brown for the eyebrows
* Yellow stranded embroidery thread to finish the dress
* Red crayon to colour the cheeks
* Fray Check crystals
* Liquid Fray Check or clear nail polish

Making the rag doll

Trace the pattern for the rag doll given on page 88 and use it to make a card template (see page 9). Cut out the doll following the instructions in step 1 overleaf and stitch her together following the instructions given, using backstitch for seams and ladder stitch for closing seams (see page 10).

1 *Preparing the pattern* Use Fray Check crystals to treat the rag doll fabric following the manufacturer's instructions and leave to dry thoroughly. Now fold the fabric in half and work a few lines of tacking stitches to hold it securely down the middle and across the width. Place the template on the fabric and draw round it but do not cut out the rag doll at this stage. Backstitch all round the figure, stitching on the line you have drawn. When you have sewn all round, cut out the rag doll ⅛in (3mm) outside the sewing line.

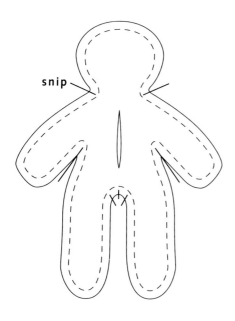

snip

2 *Turning the doll out* Make a snip close to the stitching line under the arms, between the legs and at both sides of the neck/head, as shown. This stops the seams from puckering at these points when it is turned right sides out. Draw a line of clear nail polish or Fray Check along the slit line on the back of the doll's body and allow to dry well. Cut the slit, being very careful to cut through just one thickness of fabric. Now turn the rag doll right sides out through the slit.

3 *Stuffing and shaping the doll* The doll is now ready to stuff. Only a very small amount of stuffing is required – it is important not to over-stuff the limbs. Insert a small amount of stuffing into the legs, fold the feet up and ladder stitch to the legs. Work a line of backstitch across the top of the legs. Now stuff the arms

Actual-size pattern for the rag doll

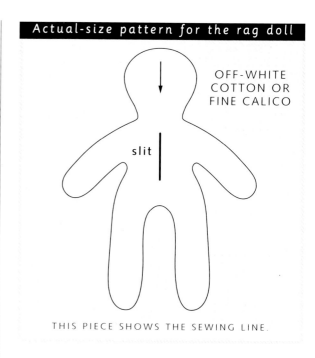

OFF-WHITE COTTON OR FINE CALICO

slit

THIS PIECE SHOWS THE SEWING LINE.

and topstitch across the top in the same way to define the body. Carefully stuff the body and when you are happy with the stuffing close the back seam with ladder stitch. To shape the neck wrap a piece of thread tightly round the dolls' neck and knot at the back of the head. Do the same round the wrists to give her hands.

4 *Adding the hair* Cut approximately ten 2½in (6.5cm) lengths of brown stranded embroidery thread. Thread your needle with one long strand of the

same colour and tie a knot at the end. Insert the needle into the dolls' head and come out at the centre front. Take one of the cut lengths, place it centrally on the head and then take a stitch over it. Continue to add the stranded embroidery thread in this manner until her hair is complete. Tie into two bunches with narrow ribbon and trim the length as required.

5 *Embroidering the face* The dolls' face is embroidered using one strand of stranded embroidery thread. Using black or dark navy blue work a French knot for each eye. Start and end at the back of the head so that the knots can be lost in the hair. For the nose work two small parallel stitches facing downwards with light pink thread, losing the ends of the thread in the hair as before. Work the mouth with two or three backstitches in red. For her eyebrows stitch a single backstitch and then anchor it down in the centre using brown. For her rosy cheeks simply apply a little bit of red crayon.

6 *Making the dress* Take a 2⅗in (6.5cm) length of yellow satin ribbon ⅝in (1.5cm) wide. Cut 1in (2.5cm) down the centre and cut a tiny circle at the end. As the ribbon will fray badly, treat this immediately with clear nail varnish or liquid Fray Check and leave to dry

well. Place over the rag dolls' neck with the cut end down her back. Stitch the end in place on her front, then turn the doll over and stitch the centre of the ribbon down her back. Anchor the end of the ribbon in place on her back. Do not stitch the sides of the ribbon – if the ribbon is standing up too much on her shoulders, pinch it together on the back of the doll at the waist and stitch in place.

7 *Making the skirt and underskirt* Take a 4in (10cm) length of cream ribbon and with right sides together join the two ends using backstitch. Work small running stitch along one edge of the ribbon and gently pull the stitches up. Fit round the dolls' waist and secure the running stitch. Repeat this with yellow ribbon for the skirt, then cover the seam with a length of matching braid or ribbon and stitch in place. Finally, tie a length of matching yellow embroidery thread round her neck to finish the dress.

TIP – Using narrow ribbon

When using narrow ribbon pass the cut end over a lit match to seal it. This prevents the end from fraying which makes it much easier to work with.

MINI TEDDIES

We all need a teddy to take to bed. Even Bedtime Bear has two miniature companions to snuggle and cuddle at night – Baby Bear who is just 1½in (4cm) tall and the even smaller Tiny Ted who stands just 1in (2.5cm) high. Being so small, these bears are very quick to make – perhaps all your teddies would like one.

Baby Bear is made in the conventional way but Tiny Ted is so small that the pieces are stitched together from the outside so that there is no need to turn the tiny limbs out. He does not have any paws or foot pads either. Both bears are thread jointed rather than using 'T' pin fibreboard cotter pin joints which are too large.

Making Baby Bear

Trace the pattern pieces for Baby Bear, given opposite, and use them to make card templates (see page 9). Transfer the paws and pads onto a single layer of ultra suede and cut out, adding an ⅛in (3mm) seam allowance around each piece. Transfer the remaining pieces onto the wrong side of a single layer of miniature bear fabric with the arrow on the pattern pointing in the direction of the fabric pile. Cut out the pieces, adding an ⅛in (3mm) seam allowance around each one. Make the bear following the instructions below, using backstitch for seams and ladder stitch for closing seams (see page 10).

TWO VERSIONS OF TINY TED WITH BABY BEAR IN THE MIDDLE
FINISHED HEIGHTS 1 AND 1½IN (2.5 AND 4CM)
(SHOWN HERE LARGER THAN ACTUAL SIZE)

You will need

+ 6 x 5in (15 x 13cm) piece of miniature bear fabric (American upholstery fabric, short-pile mohair or soft upholstery fabric) for each bear
+ Matching ultra suede for Baby Bear's paws and pads
+ General-purpose sewing thread to match the bear fabric
+ Black general-purpose sewing thread
+ Black stranded embroidery thread for the nose
+ Black ultra suede for the nose
+ Darning and fine sharp needles
+ Polyester filling
+ Pair of matching black seed beads for eyes for each bear
+ Beeswax
+ Narrow silk ribbon for a neck bow

1 *Getting started* Join the body pieces and make the arms in the same way as for Goldie, steps 1-2 (page 13). Fold each leg in half lengthways with right sides together and sew round the top of the leg from A to B. Work an extra stitch to take you round the corner and to avoid a square top of the leg. Then sew the top of the foot from C to D but leave your needle and thread attached. Attach the foot pad following the instructions for Goldie, step 4 (page 14), then continue following the steps for Goldie to make the head and to add the eyes.

2 *Preparing the head* Thread your needle with quite a long length of matching thread and knot both ends together to make a double thread. Run it across beeswax to give it extra strength and then work small running stitches around the head opening. Pull up the running stitch so the opening is completely closed. Knot the thread but do not cut off the end; set to one side. Fill the

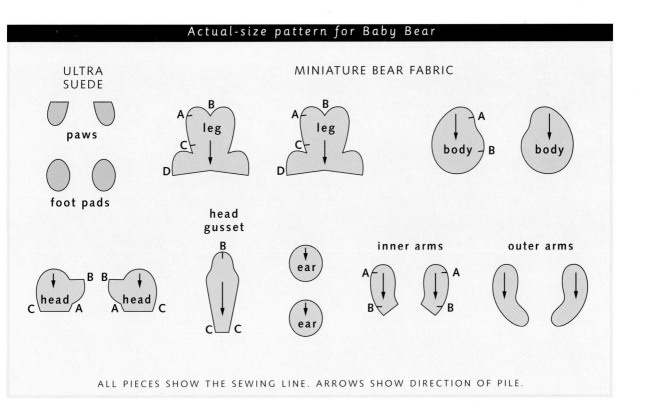

Actual-size pattern for Baby Bear

ULTRA SUEDE

MINIATURE BEAR FABRIC

paws

foot pads

head

head gusset

leg

leg

body

body

ear

ear

inner arms

outer arms

ALL PIECES SHOW THE SEWING LINE. ARROWS SHOW DIRECTION OF PILE.

body and limbs, taking care not to over-fill them because they are so small. Close all the seams with ladder stitch.

3 *Thread-jointing the head* Put a pin through the top of the bear's head and position the head on the body. Using the needle and thread already attached to the head put the needle into the top of the body where the pin is and bring it out at the bottom of the bear's body. Put the needle back in exactly the same hole that it came out of and bring it out again at the top of the bear's head, just behind one of the ears. Put the needle back in exactly the same place, go through the neck and body and bring it out again at the bottom of the body. Repeat this again, bringing the needle out just behind the other ear. Finally, take the needle through the body again and finish off the thread at the bottom of the body. This should be sufficient to secure the head. If you feel it still needs another few stitches, just repeat the stitching.

4 *Positioning the limbs* Use four pins to mark the positions of the arms and legs. Make sure that the tops of the arms are level and are positioned more towards the back of the body than the front. The legs should line up directly under the arm positions and be a little way up from the bottom of the body. Check the tops of the bear's legs are level and that he will be able to stand up straight and sit correctly.

5 *Thread-jointing the limbs* Run a 20in (51cm) length of matching thread across beeswax to strengthen it and thread a darning needle. Following the instructions for William, step 4, thread-joint the arms and legs (see page 25). Then use one strand of black embroidery thread to give your bear a nose by working small satin stitches in the shape of a V. Follow step 16 on page 18 to add the mouth. As the bear is so small make sure you don't make the nose or mouth too big. Finally, trim Baby Bear with a tiny bow round his neck made from narrow silk ribbon.

Actual-size pattern for Tiny Ted

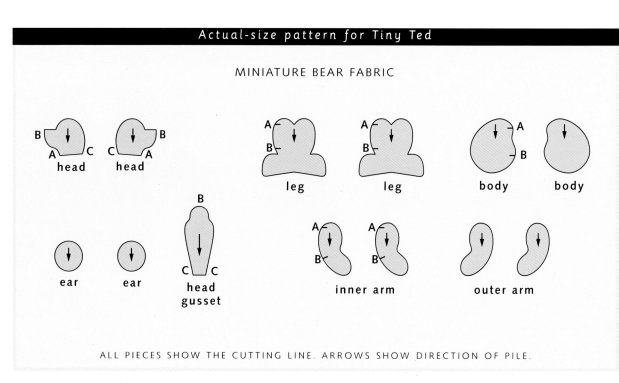

ALL PIECES SHOW THE CUTTING LINE. ARROWS SHOW DIRECTION OF PILE.

Making Tiny Ted

Trace the pattern pieces for Tiny Ted given on the previous page and use them to make card templates (see page 9). Transfer the pieces onto the wrong side of a single layer of miniature bear fabric with the arrow on the pattern pointing in the direction of the fabric pile. Cut out the pieces, without adding a seam allowance. Make the bear as explained here, by oversewing from the right side (see page 10). Enlarge the pattern slightly to make a bigger Ted.

Make Tiny Ted in the same way as Baby Bear (see pages 91-92) but do not stitch the pieces with right sides facing because they are too small to turn. Instead work all the pieces from the outside, oversewing the seams with tiny stitches. Tiny Ted does not have any paws or pads so when you make his arms and legs simply stitch all round each piece, leaving a gap for filling, then stuff the limbs and close the gap.

BIRTH CERTIFICATE

It's nice to make an official record of the 'birth' of your bear by creating your own birth certificate. You can keep it with your bear or make one to accompany him on his travels so he never loses touch with his origins.

Use a colour photocopier to make a copy of the certificate below or generate your own, either on a computer or directly on paper. If you photocopy a blank certificate for each bear you can add details and personal embellishments as desired.

Certificate of Birth

This certifies that

was born on

Beautifully handmade by

ACKNOWLEDGEMENTS

I would like to thank all my family and friends for their generous support and assistance, all of whom made writing this miniature bear collection possible. I would particularly like to express my gratitude to my assistant Gill Marshall and also to international bear artists Wendy and Megan Chamberlain. I would like to thank my husband Mark, my children James and Hilary, my mother Joyce Gray and also Sue and Adam Hands for their patience and support while I wrote this book. In addition I would like to thank the following suppliers for their generosity: Maggie Spackman of Minikins, Linda Wilson of Chapel Crafts, Lyndel Smith and Susan Lee.

Finally I would like to thank Alan Duns for the superb photography, Cheryl Brown, Sue Cleave, Betsy Hosegood, Brenda Morrison, Sandra Pruski and all the team at David & Charles publishers who made this book possible.

SUPPLIERS AND CONTACTS

There is an ever-growing list of suppliers for miniature bear fabrics, tools and accessories. The companies listed below all offer an efficient mail order service. When requesting catalogues or further information it is recommended you telephone first as there may be a small charge for catalogues/samples.

Julie K. Owen
The Great British Bear Company
10 Malleson Road
Gotherington
CHELTENHAM
Glos GL52 9ER
Mobile: 07850 505058
Tel/Fax: 01242 675000
email: julie@greatbritishbears.com
www.greatbritishbears.com

Details: everything you need for making miniature teddy bears! Supplier of a wide range of fabrics, needles, threads, eyes, joints, fillings etc including most of those used for making the bears illustrated in this book. Also good-quality bear making tools including forceps, long-nose tweezers and small cotter keys, all invaluable when making miniatures, and all the components needed for armature.

Roberta Kasnick Ripperger
Creative Design Studio
511 Berkley,
ELMHURST, II
60126 3728
USA
Details: designer of the armature method used in this book. Contact the Great British Bear Co. for supplies.

Susan Lee
8, Springfields,
TETBURY,
Glos   GL8 8EN
Tel. 01666 505936
Details: Susan Lee has a wide range of superb quality $\frac{1}{12}$ scale hand-crafted leather footwear, accessories and nursery toys. She very kindly loaned the toys for the $\frac{1}{12}$ scale nursery scene and also made the tiny ballet shoes on pages 49 and 50.

Carrie Attwood
Littlebloomers
2 Witley Avenue
HALESOWEN
West Midlands B63 4DN
www.littlebloomers.freeserve.co.uk

Wendy and Megan Chamberlain
Essential Bears
20 Belmont Road
Mowbray
CAPE TOWN, South Africa
email: ebears@iafrica.com
http://users.iafrica.com/e/eb/ebears

Lyndel Smith
27 Bragbury End,
STEVENAGE,
Herts   SG2 8TJ
Tel. 01438 813981
Details: Lyndel Smith produces a wide range of beautiful $\frac{1}{12}$ scale individually hand-painted furniture. She very kindly loaned the furniture used for the $\frac{1}{12}$ scale nursery scene.

Maggie Spackman of Minikins
51, Fotherley Road,
Mill End,
RICKMANSWORTH,
Herts   WD3 2QQ
Tel. 01923 447147
www.maggiesminikins.fsnet.co.uk
Details: Maggie Spackman of Minikins designed and knitted the outfit for the skier on page 67. She makes a wonderful range of award-winning bears, many of them wearing hand-knitted clothes.

Linda Wilson
Chapel Crafts,
The Chapel,
Benningholme Lane,
Skirlaugh,
HULL   HU11 5EA
Tel. 01964 562867
Details: supplier of Fray Check crystals to treat mohair and other fabrics. This method of fray-proofing is most effective and used extensively when making the mohair bears for this book.

MAGAZINES

There are several magazines for the teddy bear enthusiast which also include articles on miniature bears, plus details of suppliers and teddy bear fairs. Many of the magazines are available on subscription or from newsagents, including W.H. Smith.

The Teddy Bear Club International
Aceville Publications Ltd.,
Castle House,
97, High Street,
COLCHESTER,
Essex   CO1 1TH
Tel. 01454 620070 for subscriptions
Tel 01206 505979 – Lorna Floyde, editor
Details: a magazine for arctophiles with a world-wide circulation. The Teddy Bear Club International is a monthly magazine which provides patterns and information on making bears of all size and there are regular interviews with top miniature bear artists.

Teddy Bear Scene (& Other Furry Friends)
EMF House,
5-7, Elm Park,
FERRING,
West Sussex   BN12 5RN
Tel. 01903 244900
www.dolltedemf@aol.com
Details: a specialist publication for the teddy bear enthusiast. They also organise teddy bear fairs including one at Alexandra Palace and one at the N.A.C., Stoneleigh, nr. Coventry.

Teddy Bear Times
Avalon Court, Star Road,
PARTRIDGE GREEN,
West Sussex   RH13 8RY
Tel. 01403 711511
Fax. 01403 711521
Details: publishers of a monthly teddy bear magazine which is widely available from major newsagents. Organisers of the Annual British Bear Fair, early December in Hove, East Sussex and also the Teddy Bear Fair at the Business Design Centre in London at Easter.

INDEX